MARKET NEUTRAL

THE IRWIN
ASSET ALLOCATION SERIES
FOR INSTITUTIONAL
INVESTORS

MARKET NEUTRAL

State-of-the-Art Strategies for Every Market Environment

Edited by
JESS LEDERMAN and ROBERT A. KLEIN

IRWIN
Professional Publishing®
Chicago • London • Singapore

Times Mirror
Higher Education Group

Library of Congress Cataloging in Publication Data

Market neutral: state-of-the-art strategies for every market
    environment   /
Jess Lederman, Robert A. Klein, editors.
        p. cm. — (The Irwin asset allocation series for
institutional investors)
    ISBN 0-7863-0733-1
    1. Speculation. 2. Investment analysis.   I. Lederman, Jess
II. Klein, Robert A. (Robert Arnold), 1953–   .   III. Series.
HG6015.M25   1996
332.63'228—dc20   96–487

Printed in the United States of America
1 2 3 4 5 6 7 8 9 0 BS 3 2 1 0 9 8 7 6

To Bill and Gloria Newton,
and to Richard and Jayne Johnston
for their outstanding support of the
Jackson Hole Community Housing Trust

PREFACE

The Irwin Asset Allocation Series for Institutional Investors is dedicated to exploring both the theory and real-world application of cutting-edge topics. *Market Neutral* follows *Hedge Funds* and *Equity Style Management* as the third book in this exciting and innovative series.

While the theory of market-neutral investment has been around for decades, it did not come into use by more than a handful of institutions until the past few years. Indeed, it was not until 1995 that the IRS ruling that long/short positions do not create unrelated business taxable income (UBTI) cleared away the last obstacles to investment by tax-exempt investors.

By their very nature, market-neutral investment strategies tend to involve leverage and complexity, thus assuring that their implementation will generate controversy. Some well-publicized failures have involved funds that promoted themselves as market neutral, adding further fuel to the fire. And yet, at its core, market-neutral investing promises higher returns and minimal risk. So how can institutions get beyond the hype, understand the theories, and discover how to successfully adapt market-neutral techniques to their investing strategy?

Market Neutral, the first book ever compiled on this important new technique, provides the answers. The result of many months of effort by 12 of the brightest and most successful experts in the field, it covers every aspect of the subject, including concept, implementation, international applications, and operations. No finance professional who wants to understand the contemporary investment landscape should be without it.

Many thanks are owed to each of the contributing authors for the time and energy they took from their hectic schedules. Thanks is also owed to the superb staff at Irwin Professional Publishing, who made the timely publication of this important book possible.

Jess Lederman
Robert A. Klein

Contents

Chapter 5

Alternative Quantitative Approaches to Long/Short Strategies   73
Russell J. Brooks, Principal, Market Profile Theorems, Inc.

Chapter 6

Using a Nonparametric Approach to Market-Neutral Investing   93
Geoffrey Gerber, President, Twin Capital Management, Inc.

Chapter 10

Domestic Custodial Issues   165
Jane E. Sinclair, Western Regional Director, Neuberger & Berman

Chapter 11

Global Custody Issues   177
Richard Portogallo, Managing Director, Morgan Stanley & Co.
Incorporated

AUTHOR BIOGRAPHIES

Russell J. Brooks

Mr. Brooks is a founder and principal of Market Profile Theorems, Inc., a company that provides quantitative investment research, particularly in the area of style management. Additionally, his firm has formed joint ventures that manage a variety of alternative quantitative strategies. Prior to founding Market Profile Theorems, Mr. Brooks had 27 years experience in providing investment research to institutional money managers and plan sponsors. He has testified before the U.S. House of Representatives on the subject of "soft dollars," and has given numerous speeches nationwide on that subject.

Jane Buchan

Ms. Buchan is a director and portfolio manager with Collins Associates, and is responsible for market-neutral products and for research on quantitative strategies and asset allocation. Previously, she worked at J.P. Morgan Investment Management in the capital markets research group.

Ms. Buchan holds a B.A. in Economics from Yale University and is working on her Ph.D. from Harvard in Business Economics.

Geoffrey Gerber

Dr. Gerber is the chief executive officer and chief investment officer of Twin Capital Management, Inc. Previously, he was senior vice president and head of quantitative analysis and systems for Mellon Equity Associates and was a director at Prudential Asset Management Company.

Dr. Gerber holds a Ph.D. in Finance and Economics from the University of Pennsylvania and a B.A. in Economics from the State University of New York at Buffalo.

Martin J. Gross

Mr. Gross is president of Sandalwood Securities, Inc. He tracks hedge funds and advises onshore and offshore funds of funds from Livingston, New Jersey. A member of the New Jersey and New York Bars, Mr. Gross has practiced tax and corporate law and worked in the corporate finance department of L.F. Rothschild, Unterberg, & Towbin. He has written for Barron's and for hedge fund newsletters and often lectures at industry conferences.

Mr. Gross received a B.A. in Philosophy summa cum laude from Brandeis University, an M.A. from Brasenose College, Oxford University, a J.D. from the University of Chicago Law School, and an LL.M. from New York University Law School.

David Krider

Mr. Krider is an associate with First Quadrant Corporation, where he has designed systems to streamline the portfolio management process and has been involved in nearly all elements of First Quadrant's equity management program. His work has played an important role in the integration of the research and operations aspects of equity management for First Quadrant.

Mr. Krider is a graduate of the California Institute of Technology, where he earned a dual B.S. degree in Computer Science and Economics. He is currently pursuing a Ph.D. in Finance.

Louis J. Marett

Mr. Marett is the managing partner of the tax department of the law firm Nutter, McClennen & Fish. He has over 20 years experience in the taxation of financial products. Mr. Marett is a frequent speaker and author on topics in taxation, and a trustee of the Massachusetts Taxpayers Foundation, the Schepens Eye Research Institute, and the St. Vincent de Paul Foundation.

Mr. Marett is a graduate of Harvard College, magna cum laude in Economics, and a cum laude graduate of Harvard Law School.

Richard O. Michaud

Dr. Michaud is senior vice president and director of research for Acadian Asset Management, where he focuses on asset allocation, optimization, stock valuation, portfolio strategies, and trading costs. Previously, he held positions as director of research and new product development at State Street Bank and Trust Co., as head of equity analytics at Merrill Lynch, and as director of quantiative investment services at Prudential Securities. Dr. Michaud is a director of the Q Institute and an editorial board member of the Financial Analysts Journal.

Dr. Michaud received a Ph.D. in Mathematics from Boston University and has taught investment management at Columbia University's Graduate School of Business.

Richard Portogallo

Mr. Portogallo is a managing director with Morgan Stanley & Co. Incorporated, and is responsible for all facets of Morgan Stanley's worldwide prime brokerage services. Previously, he held positions with Dean Witter Reynolds, including director of the money cashiering department.

Mr. Portogallo graduated from Saint Francis College with a B.A. in Business Administration, and received an MBA from Pace University.

Robert E. Shultz

Mr. Shultz is a consultant to both institutional and non-traditional money managers. Previously, he was a senior vice president of The Common Fund, with responsibility for domestic equity funds of $3.9 billion, and as head of research. Mr. Shultz was managing director of client relations at Trust Company of the West, and has also held positions as vice president of Pension Asset Management for RJR Nabisco, Inc., as director of U.S. retirement funds for IBM, and as pension fund administration manager for Western Electric Company. He serves on the board of directors for the Institute of Quantitative Research in Finance and on the Advisory Council of the Society of Quantitative Analysts, Inc.

Mr. Shultz holds a B.S. degree in Business Administration from Norwich University.

Jane E. Sinclair
Ms. Sinclair is western regional director for Neuberger & Berman, where she markets prime-broker services and specializes in market-neutral advisory firms. Previously, she was a managing director for Bear Stearns Security Corporation, where she opened the West Coast prime broker office and developed relationships with an emphasis on market-neutral advisors. Ms. Sinclair is a member of the Association of Investment Sales and of the Financial Women's Association of San Francisco. She is an arbitrator for the New York Stock Exchange and the National Futures Exchange and is a frequent speaker at operations and hedge fund conferences.

Peter Swank
Dr. Swank is associate director at First Quadrant Corporation, an $11 billion institutional money management firm, where he helps to develop and manage quantitatively based international equity portfolio strategies. Previously, he served on the faculty of the USC School of Business Administration. Dr. Swank serves as the president of the Los Angeles Quantitative Investment Association, and is a frequent speaker in the area of quantitative investment management.

Dr. Swank is a Phi Beta Kappa graduate of the Univesity of Illinois, where he received a B.A. in Mathematics, and received an M.A. and a Ph.D. in Economics from the University of California.

David A. White

Mr. White is executive vice president of AIG International Asset Management, Inc., where he is responsible for investment analysis, product development, manager selection, and marketing. Previously, he was treasurer and chief investment officer of The Rockefeller Foundation. Prior to that, Mr. White was staff vice president of capital management and trust investments, for Unisys Corporation, where he implemented several investment firsts, including market neutral and currency as an asset class. He is a member of the Financial Executives Institute (FEI) and was a trustee of The Investment Fund for Foundations (TIFF).

Mr. White received a B.A. in Economics and Mathematics and an M.A. in Finance and Operations from the University of Michigan.

1

⊚ INTRODUCTION TO MARKET-NEUTRAL INVESTING

David A. White
Executive Vice President
AIG International Asset Management, Inc.

Market-neutral investing is responsible for most of the significant innovations in institutional investing during the past decade. The technique, which continues to be a fertile source of controversy, has been the topic of numerous articles, books, private letter rulings, and conferences to satisfy the ongoing interest of investment professionals. Although the market-neutral investment structure is at least 45 years old, fiduciary concerns, unclear tax regulations, complexity, and Regulation "T" conspired to severely limit institutional participation until the late 1980s. At that point, a handful of pioneers and innovative investment managers overwhelmed their investment committees, lawyers, custodians, and accountants with the powerful mathematics of "double alpha" to gain approval of this "new" money management approach. Innovations at the end of the 1980s brought "equitized" and "bonditized" versions of the product to the investor. In the early 1990s, "transportable" alpha became a topic for discussion as return seekers recognized the independence of alpha and capital-market risk premiums and began to allocate their scarce capital to high-alpha areas without compromising long-term asset allocation policies. The range of asset classes in which market-neutral strategies have been developed includes equities, convertible securities, high-yield bonds, fixed-income securities, currencies, and other asset classes.

Market-neutral investing suffers from the three attributes that most often gave fiduciaries pause in the mid-1990s: leverage, complexity, and derivatives. Consequently, the growth of market neutral, rapid in the early 1990s, slowed to a snail's pace by the mid-1990s. While some have hailed the strategy as the most important innovation of the last 10 years, others have argued fervently that the strategy cannot add value—ever. Chapter 3 expands on the first theme, and Chapter 4 builds the case that market-neutral strategies are not superior. After a wildly successful introduction in the late 1980s, with double-digit alphas going to the first entrants, investors discovered by the early 1990s that alpha was as elusive in market neutral as in long-only strategies.

In 1994, David Askin's market-neutral, mortgage-backed-securities funds collapsed, raising concerns in board rooms across the nation. Institutional plan sponsors, as if in a McCarthy-like hunt for Communists, rooted out derivatives, leverage, and complexity in their investment programs, or ran for cover while the fiduciary police reviewed investment programs to identify and flush out the three fatal sins. Does giving a manager the three tools (leverage, derivatives, and complexity) which have been deeply involved in investing's biggest disasters of the 1990s create conditions under which the probability of manager self-destruction could increase well beyond the carefully tested simulations? Can market-neutral strategies be controlled to prevent meltdowns?

MARKET-NEUTRAL STRATEGY

In the framework of the capital asset pricing model, market-neutral investing can be described as zero beta investing. In the language of fixed-income strategies, market-neutral portfolios have a duration of zero. With duration and beta of zero, market-neutral strategies are designed to produce returns independent of capital markets. For example, in equity strategies a market-neutral portfolio holds equal amounts of long- and short-equity securities. In bond strategies, the market-neutral portfolio might be long mortgage securities and short Treasury securities, and/or complex mortgage and interest-rate derivatives to create a zero-duration portfolio.[1]

The basic market-neutral equity strategy starts with one dollar of capital, purchases a long position, and sells a stock short. The cash proceeds from the short sale are invested to produce a return that approximates the risk-free rate. Thus, the return to the strategy is the sum of the two alphas and the risk-free rate. If alpha is positive, the investor will enjoy *two* alphas, one each from the long and short portfolio. In contrast, in long-investment portfolios, which have market exposure, the investor receives a *single* alpha plus the market return, which is the asset class risk premium plus the risk-free rate. Moreover, with leverage—a topic discussed in more detail later—alpha multiples of 40 or 50 can be achieved in some market-neutral strategies.

Most market-neutral accounts hold a diversified portfolio of long positions hedged with a diversified portfolio of short positions. The resulting portfolio is designed to take advantage of anomalies between directly or indirectly related securities and/or derivatives, rather than directional moves. Other factors such as sector, industry, credit quality, price/earnings ratio, capitalization, optionality, and so forth can, in theory, be controlled to expose investor capital only to the return-generating element of the investment strategy. Market neutral encompasses a wide range of arbitrage and relative-value techniques in virtually every asset class that owes its returns largely to a manager's skill in identifying value and constructing hedges.

---

1. Note that, in practice, it has proven difficult to control risk. More will be said on this later.

A BRIEF HISTORY OF MARKET NEUTRAL

Market-neutral investing was a central element of the A. W. Jones 1949 investment partnership, sometimes referred to as the first hedge fund. In Jones's fund, a portion of the portfolio was composed of equal amounts of long and short stock, with the balance held long and exposed to the market. The "within the hedge" portion of the A. W. Jones's hedge fund was the precursor of today's market-neutral portfolios.

In 1967, Thorpe and Kassouf, in *Beat the Market,* outlined a program of systematic stock/warrant arbitrage. In their strategy, the portfolio contained long undervalued stock and short overpriced warrants. If the proportion of warrants to stock were maintained properly, it would be possible to extract the warrant's option premium, produce higher income, and post lower volatility than a long stock portfolio.

In 1973, the Black-Scholes option-pricing model was defined and the Chicago Board Options Exchange was created, allowing more investors to participate in option hedging. In 1977, futures contracts on long Treasuries were introduced, making market-neutral investing possible in fixed-income markets. Major Wall Street firms began going long futures and short Treasuries to extract the value difference between the two instruments. Basis trading grew rapidly. In 1982, the Kansas City Board of Trade introduced cash-settled futures, which reduced transactions costs and broadened the types of basis trading or futures arbitrage.

In 1987, Morgan Stanley established a quantitative group, under Nunzio Tartaglia, which engaged in equity pairs trading (for example, long Unisys, short IBM) within the net capital rules of a broker-dealer. Under these rules, leverage could be increased beyond the 2:1 (one long and one short for one dollar of capital) maximum margin financing available to non-broker-dealer customers, including pension plans and other institutional investors. The cheap stock was purchased and the rich one sold short. Because of higher leverage, higher multiples of alpha could be produced.

Finally, in 1987, after a five-year bull market in U.S. equities, the stock market crashed, reminding investors that equities do have risk. Relative value was transformed into market neutral and was seen to be a better way to invest, avoid equity risk, and earn strong returns.

In 1988, the Common Fund (which is a nonprofit consortium that manages in excess of $17 billion for over 1300 educational institutions) received an Internal Revenue Service (IRS) private letter ruling which held that short sales did not create unrelated business taxable income (UBTI). On the basis of this private letter ruling, institutional participation in market-neutral investing began. In 1995, the IRS issued the long-awaited revenue ruling (IRB 1995–4 #29) that long/short investing does not create UBTI, clearing away any lingering taxation issues.

AN EFFICIENT USE OF CAPITAL

One of the attractive features of market-neutral investing is that capital can be allocated to produce multiple alphas and, therefore, improve the return potential of investor capital. In long investment strategies, since the capital is not leveraged, only one alpha can be achieved. In theory, there is no limit to the number of alphas that could be earned on a market-neutral portfolio because the capital can be leveraged to produce multiple alphas. In practice, leverage is limited by credit providers for all classes of securities except U.S. equities, and for equities in the United States by Regulation "T."

If we think of a market-neutral portfolio in the context of a balance sheet, then the way credit markets limit leverage ratios becomes clearer. In a market-neutral portfolio with assets equal to liabilities, the amount of capital required by credit providers to support the balance sheet will determine the leverage ratio. The closer the match between assets and liabilities, the lower the net capital required. Conversely, the greater the deviation in the behavior of assets and liabilities, the higher the capital required to support the balance sheet. Thus, a strategy that has assets invested in long-duration securities and that is financed (liabilities) with short-term instruments will need a higher amount of capital than a duration-matched set of assets and liabilities. In the 1970s, the U.S. banking system proved to be undercapitalized and unable to support the mismatch in durations between assets and liabilities. In that case, the portfolio was not market neutral, since net assets and liabilities did not have a duration of zero.

A market-neutral investment account's net capital requirement is determined by the broker-dealer financing the strategy. In U.S. equities, Regulation "T" defines the maximum as 50 percent; thus, the maximum leverage is 2:1— one long and one short for one dollar of capital. In the unregulated fixed income, leverage is negotiated between the account and the broker-dealer's credit or margin department. Since Regulation "T" applies only to customer accounts, some aggressive institutional investors have established passive broker-dealers (passive to avoid taxation) in order to take advantage of the more advantageous net capital rules applied to exchange members and broker-dealers. In U.S. equities, current Securities and Exchange Commission (SEC) regulations allow broker-dealers' long/-short equity accounts to attain leverage ratios of 6.29 to 1. In convertible bonds, leverage of roughly 20:1 can be achieved. In foreign equity markets, which are not restricted by U.S.-style regulations, "contracts for differences" with local investment banks allow the attainment of equity long/short leverage ratios of up to 10:1, depending on the strategy and the overall creditworthiness of the borrower.

The mathematics of leveraged market-neutral means that alpha-only strategies can be competitive with other investments, even if the alpha is low. If a stable, low-risk market-neutral alpha of, say, 1 percent can be extracted from the capital markets, then leverage of 6:1 will make this approach competitive with the long-term equity risk premiums. Since the return is a result of manager skill, it should be uncorrelated with capital market returns, which is an added benefit.

TYPES OF MARKET-NEUTRAL STRATEGIES

The first institutional implementation of market-neutral investing in the late 1980s was the long/short equity strategy, leveraged one long and one short. Since then, the breadth of market-neutral strategies has expanded to encompass virtually every country's capital market in every asset class. Clearly, market neutral is *not* risk neutral; the technique has not altered the fundamental equation that an investor has to assume risk to earn excess return. Importantly, market-neutral investing can concentrate on promising value-added sources, hedge unwanted risks, and increase the efficiency of capital better than traditional approaches. But the strategy cannot produce alpha where there is none.

There is a continuum of market-neutral strategies ranging from low risk and high market-neutrality to high risk and low market-neutrality. Proponents believe market neutral's risks will be less volatile (risky) than market risk, even though risk in market-neutral portfolios has more dimensions than duration and beta, two principal measures of market risk. The central concept is maximum return from skill and low systematic correlation to the underlying capital market. One end of the spectrum might be long and short (within a single country) equal dollar amounts of common stocks within one industry, where the key risks will be limited almost entirely to specific company risks. At the other end of the spectrum might be a complex mortgage arbitrage trade, where management of prepayment, interest-rate, convexity, and option-volatility risks are the keys to success. Some observers might even include directional relative-value trades such as long British bonds and short S&P 500 futures as a market neutral, under the theory that the strategy encompasses no consistent long or short directional exposure, only high-probability relative-value trading.

Descriptions of seven major market-neutral categories should give potential investors a basic understanding of the range, complexity, and risks of market neutral investing.

The categories are long/short equity, capital structure arbitrage, futures arbitrage, fixed-income arbitrage, options arbitrage, risk arbitrage, and currency arbitrage.

Long/Short Equity

The long/short equity strategy entails holding offsetting portfolios of long and short equity positions, structured to eliminate the influence of the general market. A long portfolio which closely tracks a broad index such as the S&P 500 can be turned into a market-neutral portfolio by selling S&P 500 futures equal to the value of the long portfolio. Performance would be a function of the manager's stock-selection skill plus the discount rate in the S&P 500 futures, which will approximate short-term T-bill rates. The portfolio will have a low beta and show a pattern of returns uncorrelated with the equity market.

The preponderance of market-neutral equity managers sell individual stocks short, not futures contracts, to produce two alphas, one each from the long and short portfolios. There are many variations on this basic structure: dollar neutral or equal dollars long and short; sector neutral or dollar neutral with balanced sector weightings on both sides; industry specialized or long and short within one industry such as bank stocks or utilities; and beta neutral or equal betas on the long and short sides to prevent residual positive or negative betas in the aggregate portfolios. Investment managers have created endless variations on this theme, employing BARRA optimizers and other risk management tools to limit exposure to the factor which generates excess returns.

Capital Structure Arbitrage

In convertible securities arbitrage, designed to earn the positive difference between the interest on the convertible bond less the common-stock dividend which is owed to the supplier of the short stock, the convertible is purchased long and the common stock sold short. To produce returns competitive with the 6 percent long-term equity risk premium, leverage of approximately 4:1 or 5:1 is typically used (leverage measured as longs divided by capital). A successful convertible arbitrage strategy will deliver the positive spread between the convertible interest and common dividend only if the fluctuations in the long and short portfolios, in response to interest rates, equity market expectations, or option premium volatilities, offset one another. The buying and selling of common stock to maintain portfolio value is generally a dynamic model-based process; thus, convertible strategies are subject to "model" risk—the risk of a misspecified model. In unsuccessful strategies, the convertible and common will not rise and fall together, and will therefore deplete the positive cash flow advantage of the trade.

In high-yield bond arbitrage, common stock is sold short against the high-yield bond. High-yield securities are "near"-equity substitutes and are just above equity in seniority if there are no convertible securities in the capital structure. The objective is to earn the yield premium of the fixed-income instrument over the return to the common stock, hedged for changes in credit quality, interest rates, and equity price. Since the high-yield security is sensitive to the same factors that drive the equity security, high-yield bonds and common stock will have a high correlation. As with convertible securities arbitrage, the trick is to manage the ratio of high yield to common, such that the values of the long and short portfolios move closely together. Poor management of the hedge (model risk again) will be damaging to the performance of the strategy.

Futures Arbitrage

Futures arbitrage can be undertaken in equity and fixed-income markets, both domestic and foreign. The strategy is to buy long the undervalued instrument and sell short the overvalued instrument. Usually the market-index future is purchased and the basket of stocks making up the index is sold short. In fixed-income markets, leverage can be as high as 50 or 60 times. Futures arbitrage can also be performed in commodities markets, where the trade usually is long the commodity and short the index. There is risk in the commodities side because of the problems of physical storage and quality of the commodity owned. Risk in fixed-income financial futures arises because the cheapest-to-deliver bond to satisfy the settlement of the bond future may change or be subject to a short squeeze. Because the future and the underlying securities must converge to the same value (or be delivered), futures arbitrage is sometimes referred to as a convergence trade.

Fixed-Income Arbitrage

Fixed-income arbitrage has as many variations as equity market-neutral strategies. Government debt can be hedged with over-the-counter swaps, futures, or government agency or corporate bonds. In the $2.2 trillion U.S. mortgage-backed securities market—perhaps an ideal sector for market-neutral strategies because of the complex nature of the securities—the general strategy is long mortgages, hedged for interest-rate, volatility, and prepayment risks with Treasury securities or packages of complex interest-rate and option derivatives. In yield-curve arbitrage, predictions of the future shape of the yield curve are expressed in portfolios as long the cheap part of the curve and short the rich part of the curve. Yield-curve trades are not exposed to parallel shifts in interest rates, but can produce major losses if the shape of the yield curve twists the opposite of the prediction. Indeed, some observers, due to the large, unexpected losses in yield-curve arbitrage in 1995, have concluded that the strategy is not a market-neutral one. The widening and narrowing of the corporate-to-Treasuries spread can be played by taking a position in Treasuries and an offsetting position in Eurodollars. In this trade, risk is limited to movements in the spread the opposite of the prediction, because duration and yield-curve exposure are fairly easily controlled.

Most industry databases include these two capital structure arbitrage strategies under the convertible-securities caption, because convertible-abitrage managers control approximately 90 percent of the capital in this category.

Options Arbitrage

Option equivalents, a popular U.S. form of options arbitrage, is long calls and short puts (the equivalent of a long stock position) hedged with the underlying stocks or an optimized stock basket. Japanese warrant arbitrage is the long purchase of warrants and short sale of the underlying stock. The hedge ratio must be managed successfully to add value.

Risk Arbitrage

Risk arbitrage is the purchase of stock in a company that is to be acquired and the short sale of the package of cash or securities offered by the acquirer, which will be received by the target's shareholders on completion of the merger. In the case of stock for stock mergers or takeovers, the most typical case, the portfolio is long the target's common stock (the acquired company) and short the purchaser's in the proportions specified in the merger agreement. Typically, the target company's stock sells at a discount to the value of the securities to be received at the merger's closing to reflect the two principal risks that, first, the deal may not close or, second, may extend beyond the announced date. Should the merger not occur, the shares of the target can drop to pre-merger levels, sometimes 20–40 percent below the acquisition price. Risk arbitrage managers generally initiate positions after announcement, but some managers may buy stocks in anticipation of a merger or include in their portfolios a portion of these more speculative pre-announcement deals. The strategy performs best when bidding wars occur, driving the target's price above the level of the first offer. Successful merger arbitrage managers must be skilled in anti-trust law, anti-takeover defense, and shareholders' rights to correctly manage the risks of the strategy.

Currency Arbitrage

Two types of currency arbitrage became popular in the early 1990s. In open-interest arbitrage, high-interest-rate currencies are purchased and low-interest-rate currencies sold short. The resulting positive carry from the large interest advantage is enough to cover adverse currency price movements, which can be expected to reduce the profits somewhat. This game was popular until September 1993, when particularly extreme currency movements reawakened investors to the fact that 5 percent real-return T-bills do not exist. In another version, a basket of currencies making up the European Currency Unit (ECU) is offset by a short position in the ECU itself. In other variations on this theme, currencies "pegged" to one another can be arbitraged to earn the interest-rate differential. In higher-risk versions, less-well-coupled currencies can be held in long/short portfolios to produce multiple alphas from interest rates or currency movements.

LEVERAGE AND RISK

The early promise of market-neutral investing was to earn a decent spread over Treasuries with moderate volatility and inconsequential risk to capital. The first market-neutral simulations and risk models showed that risk could be controlled to stay within tight specifications. Unfortunately, in almost every year since 1990, investors have learned of new risks—risks the model did not identify nor control. The well-publicized demise of James C. Donahue's Denver-based Hedged Portfolio Advisors in 1990 should have been an early warning signal about the potentially fatal risks of market neutral in general, and of investing in partnerships without audits and independently verifiable periodic reporting in particular. Nonetheless, most investors and their committees were not prepared for the sudden, unexpected failures of David Askin and David Weill in 1994. Indeed, after Askin, a new risk—manager risk (that is, the risk that an investment firm may go under, taking its investors' capital with it)—was identified, classified, and added to the familiar list of risks to incorporate into committee presentations.

As leverage increases, risk increases. Investors should carefully evaluate whether risk added through leverage is superior, on a risk-adjusted basis, to the typical market-based risks found in most long-horizon institutional portfolios. As we learned in 1994 with the demise of the Askin mortgage securities strategy and Orange County's leveraged fixed-income strategy, some committees were unable to understand that risk undertaken through leverage is not substantially different from the risks to which capital is regularly exposed in pursuit of excess returns. It is easy to envision the response a committee would have to a collapse in the emerging markets portfolio if, for example, Argentina attacked Brazil. Yet the response to losses from complexity, derivatives, or leverage—important elements of most market-neutral strategies—has been far less reasoned or understood than in the case of unexpected war.

Historic data suggest that market-neutral investing is superior to traditional long bond and equities. Data provided by Collins Associates for the five-year period ended June 30, 1995, confirms that investment returns for the (five market-neutral categories) tracked by Collins (convertible, fixed-income, general, long/short, risk arbitrage) outperformed equities and bonds. Collins's "general" category includes futures, currency, and options-arbitrage strategies described above. Taken together, these strategies have attracted less capital than any of the other four. In market neutral, reward-to-risk ratios (annualized return divided by annual standard deviation) varied from a low of 2.92 in fixed income to 3.73 for equity long/short. In Collins Associates' complete market-neutral universe, the ratio was 5.14 because of low correlations between the five market-neutral strategies. In comparison, the S&P 500 equity ratio was 1.05 and the Lehman Brothers Aggregate fixed-income index was 2.27. The difference lay primarily in the volatility dimension, with all five of Collins's categories showing standard deviations below the S&P, and four of five equal to or below the Lehman index. All five categories posted better returns than the Lehman Aggregate, and three of five bested the S&P. It should be pointed out that Collins handled the collapse of David Askin's fund and removal from the fixed-income market-neutral universe by writing that firm's cumulative return down to zero in the database.

To address the impact of leverage, Collins ran a simulation increasing the leverage of the long/short equity strategy to the standard deviation of the Lehman Aggregate index. The equity long/short universe is leveraged one long, one short for each dollar of capital. If leverage is increased to 1.43 long and 1.43 short, the standard deviation of the strategy equaled the Lehman aggregate's standard deviation. Five-year returns for the Lehman aggregate were 9.41 percent and 14.37 percent for the 1.43 leveraged long/short equity, both with a standard deviation of 4.15 percent. Similar results were obtained for the three- and seven-year periods with leverage factors of 1.68 and 1.42, respectively.

Regardless of what the data show (or, according to market-neutral advocates, prove), an investor should carefully evaluate the risks specific to market neutral as compared with the more understandable risks of traditional long strategies, and make an informed judgement as to the suitability of the market-neutral investment strategy under review. As implied above, the career risk of leaving the typical mean-variance-optimized long-only path, in favor of market neutral's added controversial features— leverage, complexity, and derivatives—may be very high. Although the seven-year time period covered by the data is, statistically speaking, too short to draw firm conclusions, the data do suggest strongly that market neutral is a superior investment structure on a risk-adjusted basis.

IMPLEMENTATION

Typical implementation structures do little to satisfy skittish committees that the risks of market neutral can be overcome. Assets are often allocated to partnerships, outside of the investor's tightly controlled custody network, with 20 to 25 percent incentive-fee structures and no provision for independent investor monitoring of the portfolio. Resolution of UBTI issues for tax-exempt investors is a complex undertaking sure to test the limits of committee patience, particularly if leverage beyond one long, one short is required. Furthermore, the well-publicized failures in the 1990s vividly illustrate that downside risk can be intensified significantly by the features that make market-neutral investing attractive. The use of leverage, derivatives, and complexity to enhance returns also increases risk, which in an implosion may be catastrophic.

When assets are transferred to a custodian controlled by the manager, there may not be independent monitoring to assure that the portfolio is within guidelines and approved risk parameters. Some believe that Askin's investors could have saved a substantial portion of the losses had there been independent daily monitoring of leverage and duration, perhaps through a separate account structure. Consequently, some sponsors, managers, and consultants have established independent oversight systems that use the risk management tools developed by broker-dealers to monitor and control their proprietary trading activities. In 1995, the risk management business was growing as investors began frequently measuring exposures to monitor risk and assure themselves that exposures were within policy. Some were measuring "value at risk" daily.

Increasingly, just as with long accounts, investors are placing themselves in direct control of the market-neutral assets through separate accounts. Generally, the assets are held at a broker-dealer because most traditional custodians are unable to handle short sales and repurchase agreements. This allows the use of daily position reporting and risk management systems to enable investor monitoring and, if necessary, adjustment of exposures. In addition, as a normal part of due diligence, investors review the investment managers' internal control systems, scenario modelling capabilities, and backup systems as thoroughly as the managers' investment process to ensure the manager is unlikely to lose control of the portfolio.

The incentive fee structure is comparable to issuing an option to an investment manager which will result in great wealth if significant excess return is produced, whether by luck or skill. This structure may motivate the manager to take excessive risk to try to make the option pay off. To correct or reduce potential problems with this characteristic of the incentive fee system, two alternatives are being sought by investors. First, a maximum fee, say 6 percent of assets, is established to remove incentive to take excessive risks. Second, some investors demand that a portion of the incentive fees remain in the partnership to cushion results in down periods. In these structures, the reserved fee is credited to the investors' investment returns when, as inevitably occurs, returns do not meet objectives. Both these features should help overcome the weaknesses and perverse incentives of the old structures.

FUTURE DIRECTIONS

Although institutional plans have had experience with long/short equity market-neutral strategies, few Employee Retirement & Income Security Act (ERISA) plan investment directors, in control of "the biggest pool of money in the world," have implemented them. As a result, the investment banks, high net-worth individuals, and endowments that have continued their participation face less competition and, consequently, will enjoy better risk-adjusted returns than conventional investors.

Market-neutral investing is here to stay, even if used only by a growing fringe group of pioneers. Wealth is not created, expanded, and maintained without taking on risk. Market neutral, with its attendant leverage, complexity, and derivatives, offers investors the best hope for improving the risk-reward equation since the spread of mean variance optimization in the 1980s. The market-neutral structure is essentially a packaging technique, long the exclusive territory of investment banks' proprietary desks. Now, with the spread of advanced risk management technology, the range of investors able to enjoy superior risk-adjusted returns has increased dramatically.

2

⑥ SHORT SALES AND UNRELATED BUSINESS TAXABLE INCOME

Louis J. Marett,
Partner
Nutter, McClennen & Fish

Pension plans are often spoken of as tax exempt, but that is an exaggeration. Even pension plans are subject to the tax on unrelated business taxable income, often referred to as UBTI. As the name suggests, unrelated business taxable income results when a pension fund or other tax-exempt entity carries on a business which is unrelated to its exempt purpose. For a number of years, there was a serious question as to whether profits from short sales were UBTI, and the uncertainty deterred some pension funds from engaging in market-neutral strategies. Now the question has been resolved favorably. In January 1995, the Internal Revenue Service announced that income from short sales is not UBTI. This is expected to give market-neutral investing a significant boost. To understand why, some background is necessary.

First, keep in mind that, if an otherwise tax-exempt organization realizes UBTI, the practical consequences may vary depending upon the type of tax-exempt organization involved:

- *Universities* routinely incur UBTI from diverse activities including providing their athletic and other facilities and services to various community groups. Consequently, many university endowments would be undeterred by the prospect of realizing UBTI from their investment portfolios so long as after-tax returns were adequate.

- *Pension plans*, by contrast, do not routinely realize UBTI. Hence, realizing even a small amount of UBTI from an investment portfolio requires crossing an unfamiliar threshold: a federal return on Form 990-T must be filed and tax paid on the reported income.

- *Charitable remainder trusts* are unique in that all of their annual income will be subject to tax if any of it is comprised of UBTI. Hence, for a charitable remainder trust, the risk of incurring UBTI is very serious.

THE GENESIS OF THE TAX ON UBTI

The story of the tax on UBTI begins in the years immediately following World War II, when New York University (NYU) Law School formed a wholly owned charitable subsidiary to acquire, with borrowed funds, the pasta manufacturing business of the C. F. Mueller Company. Needless to say, this transaction set off some bells. Taxable competitors of Mueller were not amused at the cost advantage that Mueller would enjoy. Equally unamused was the U.S. Treasury, which quickly realized that, through this bootstrap technique, NYU would be able to pay off its acquisition loan with the untaxed profits of the business it had acquired. Carried to its logical conclusion, this technique would have given tax exempts an enormous advantage over taxable competitors in bidding for the acquisition of existing businesses. Indeed, it was easily foreseeable that a significant portion of U.S. business could end up in the hands of tax exempts and thus be removed from the income tax roles. The tax on UBTI quickly followed.

Under the original formulation of the rules, the income of tax exempts was subjected to the regular income tax to the extent that it was derived from a trade or business, the conduct of which was not *substantially related* to the exempt functions of the organization. Because the manufacture of pasta is not "substantially related" to the education of law students, NYU and its imitators would be subject to tax.

Tax planners were not sitting idly by, however, and they soon developed various sale-and-leaseback techniques to avoid the new tax on UBTI. Typical of the new techniques was one considered in the *Clay Brown* case[1]. This case involved an exempt organization that acquired an existing business, which it then leased to a new operating company owned by the former owners of the business. Rental payments were a major fraction of the profits of the business. These rental payments were deductible by the management company and were not taxable to the exempt organization which received them because, under existing rules, rents were (and still are in many cases) investment income rather than income from a trade or business.

The Congressional response was to provide a second general category of UBTI: income from debt-financed property. Under these rules, if a tax-exempt entity realized income from property which it incurred a debt to acquire, the income was UBTI. It is this rule which raised questions about short sales.

SHORT-SALE MECHANICS AND UBTI

To initiate a short sale, one typically phones a stock broker, who arranges to borrow shares of the company to be shorted and then sells those shares on the open market. The proceeds of the sale are then held by the broker as security for the investor's obligation to replace the borrowed

---

1. 380 US 563 (1965).

stock. While they are held by the broker, the proceeds are invested at interest, a small portion of which is retained by the broker and the balance of which is paid to the investor. At some subsequent date, the investor instructs the broker to close the short sale, at which time the broker purchases shares of the shorted company on the open market and replaces the borrowed shares. If the price of a share of the shorted company had declined at the time of the closing of the short sale, the result would be a profit. The issue is whether this profit is a profit from debt-financed property (the borrowed stock), in which event it would be UBTI.

THE INTERNAL REVENUE SERVICE RESPONSE

This question perplexed market-neutral investors, several of which asked the advice of the IRS. In 1988, the IRS issued a "private letter ruling" to one of these investors, reportedly The Common Fund, in which the IRS agreed that no UBTI resulted from a short sale.[2] The rationale of the ruling was that, because the obligation to replace the borrowed stock was fully secured by the cash proceeds of the short sale, there was no net borrowing.

Shortly thereafter, it appears that the IRS became disenchanted with this rationale, and rightly so. After all, when one buys a house, the mortgage note is typically well secured, but surely no one would suggest that there was no net borrowing. In any event, the IRS let it be known that it would undertake a study and that, pending the outcome of that study, it would issue no more rulings on this subject. Seven short years later the study was concluded, and in

---

2. Private Letter Ruling 8832052. The full text of the ruling is attached as an Appendix. The Code provides that private letter rulings may not be cited as authority by taxpayers other than the one to whom the ruling is addressed. In practice, however, taxpayers often act based on private letter rulings issued to others.

January 1995 the IRS announced once again that short sales did not produce UBTI.[3] This time, little in the way of rationale was offered except for a reference to a 1940 Supreme Court case which stated, in an almost off-hand way, that "an obligation [to return borrowed stock] is not necessarily an indebtedness."[4]

Then, to give tax advisers food for thought, the IRS promptly issued two revenue rulings which seemed to undercut the rationale of the UBTI ruling. First, the IRS ruled that short sales of securities by partnerships create partnership liabilities for many partnership purposes.[5] Then the IRS ruled that the assumption by a corporation of the obligation to replace stock which was borrowed to initiate a short sale constitutes the assumption of a liability for some corporate tax purposes.[6]

Should these seemingly contradictory rulings be of concern? The answer is no. The UBTI ruling is well founded and there is no reason to doubt its vitality. To begin with, the policy considerations which gave rise to the UBTI rules do not apply to a short sale. The tax-exempt status of an entity gives it no advantage over any other entity in executing a short sale. Moreover, short sales are initiated on established markets at market prices, and there is no reason to think that short sales by tax-exempt entities will have any greater or lesser impact on the market than short sales by taxable entities. Moreover, the *lending* of securities for purposes of short selling does not give rise to UBTI.[7] The rationale was that Congress did not intend that ordinary, routine investment activities be considered

3. Revenue Ruling 95–8. The full text of the ruling is attached as an Appendix. This is a revenue ruling, as distinguished from a private letter ruling. Revenue rulings are intended to provide guidance to all taxpayers.
4. *Deputy v. DuPont,* 308 US 488, 497 (1940).
5. Revenue Ruling 95–26.
6. Revenue Ruling 95–45.
7. Revenue Ruling 78–88; see also Code Sections 512 (b) (1), 512 (a) (5), and 514 (c) (8).

a trade or business for purposes of the UBTI rules; this rationale should apply to the short seller as well as to the lender of the security.

A further analogy is provided by short futures contracts, which the IRS has concluded do not give rise to UBTI.[8] Short futures contracts are in many respects the economic equivalent of short sales. If short futures contracts do not give rise to UBTI, then neither should short sales. After all, is it not merely an accident of history that short sales are executed as they are, by a sale of borrowed stock, rather than by contract, as in the case of short future contracts?

Indeed, while short sales are almost always initiated by the sale of borrowed stock, analysis leads to the conclusion that the borrowing serves a function of the broker, rather than of the short seller. There is no *economic* reason why a short sale cannot be executed simply by contract between the broker and the short seller. If the price of the stock declines, the broker owes the short seller a payment, and vice versa. The short seller would be perfectly happy with such a transaction and would be indifferent to whether or not stock had been borrowed and sold.

Most brokers, however, are in business to earn fees for their services rather than to take risks as principals. A broker who had entered into such a contract could transfer the risk of the long end of the contract by a simple mechanism: borrowing the stock and selling it on the open market. Then, if the stock price were to rise, the broker would be entitled to receive a payment from the short seller, and the broker could use this payment to replace the borrowed stock. By contrast, if the price of the stock were to fall, the broker would owe a payment to the short seller, which the broker could generate by replacing the borrowed stock at a profit.

It appears, therefore, that the borrowing of stock in a conventional short-sale transaction serves a *broker* func-

---

8. GCM 39620 (1987).

tion rather than an investor function. Accordingly, any profit made by the market-neutral investor cannot be attributed to a borrowing, and no UBTI should result.

The inescapable conclusion is that the IRS reached the correct result in its UBTI ruling, and no investor should be deterred from market-neutral strategies by the fear that short selling will result in UBTI.

IRS Private Letter Ruling 8832052

LTR 8832052, May 18, 1988

Symbol: E:EO:R
Uniform Issue List Nos.: 0501.26–06
0512.01–00
0514.05–0

This is in response to the letter dated August 18, 1987, submitted by your representative, in which rulings were requested in connection with your proposed investments in arbitrage positions involving stocks and securities.

The information submitted indicates that [M] is organized and operated solely to manage the investment funds of educational organizations described in clause (ii) or (iv) of section 170(b)(1)(A) of the Code. [M] has been recognized as exempt from Federal Income Tax as an organization described in sections 501(c)(3) and 501(1) of the Code.

In order to obtain a higher rate of return on its investments, [M] proposes from time to time to have investments in arbitrage positions in stocks and securities when market conditions indicate a favorable return. The proposed investments would be made when there is an advantageous price spread between the cash price of stocks or securities and either related futures contracts or put and call options.

[M] has submitted an explanation, which follows below, of the transactions to be involved in these investments. In the case of an arbitrage involving stocks and futures contracts, a typical transaction would be a sale of a group of stocks reasonably representing a stock market index that is the subject of futures contracts traded on an exchange, and the purchase of the corresponding futures contracts covering an equivalent amount of stock. When the spread between the cash price of such stocks and the equivalent futures contract is sufficient, after all expenses of the transactions, to provide an incremental rate of return to the maturity date of the futures contracts, the arbitrage position offers an attractive short-term investment opportunity.

[M] would obtain the stocks required for the sale either from its own longer-term holdings or through a collateralized loan of such stocks obtained from an independent person. Any such loans of stock would involve no net borrowings by [M] because such loans would conform to the regulations of the Securities and Exchange Commission and would be secured by cash or Treasury securities owned by [M] in an amount that is kept marked to a level that is not less than the current market price of the borrowed stocks. The purchase of futures contracts requires a margin deposit of Treasury securities or other acceptable collateral that is maintained at a level not less than a stated percentage (currently about 5 percent) of the current market value of the indexed stocks covered by the contract. The costs of the stock arbitrage positions thus involve the transaction costs for the purchases and sales of the stocks and the future contracts, the loss of part of the income with respect to the cash or securities securing the borrowed stock, and the payment to the lender of dividends relating to the borrowed stock.

On occasion, an opposite arbitrage position may become economically attractive. In such case, [M] would make a cash purchase of stocks reasonable [sic] representing a futures index and would sell the futures index. [M]'s assets would be employed to purchase the stocks and to maintain the margin required for the sale of the futures index.

Similar arbitrage positions are available involving United States Treasury Bonds, Notes, and Bills. For example, a futures contract involving Treasury Bonds is quoted in terms of an 8 percent interest return equivalent, and can be satisfied at the option of the seller by delivery of Treasury Bonds having particular characteristics, which normally would include more than one outstanding bond issue. It would usually be assumed that the financial futures contract would be satisfied by delivery of whichever of the qualified issues was trading at the lowest market price at the time of maturity of the contract. Such arbitrage positions in Treasury securities would ordinarily be effected in a manner similar to the stock arbitrage positions described above. The Treasury securities required for a sale would be obtained either from a portfolio position of [M] or through a repurchase agreement effected with an independent person secured by a deposit of cash or other Treasury securities, and the margin required for the purchase of the financial futures contract would similarly be supplied from assets of [M].

All cash or Treasury securities required for the margin accounts to support the futures contracts and for collateral security for any borrowed stock or securities would be provided from cash or securities owned by [M]. Although under some circumstances [M] would "borrow" stock or securities from independent persons in order to effect its arbitrage position, the entire market value of the stock so borrowed would at all times be covered by cash or securities deposits by [M], so that no net borrowings would at any time be made in connection with the proposed arbitrage positions.

The economic effect of hedging a long or short position in stocks comprising a traded Index with put and call options on such index is similar to hedges involving futures contracts. In the case of a "reverse conversion," stocks comprising the relevant index are sold, and this sale is hedged by buying an equivalent number of calls on the index. To reduce the net cost of the option hedge, an equivalent number of puts on the index are sold. If the relative prices of the stocks and of the put and call options are favorable (after allowances for the cost of dividends on the stocks sold) at the time the hedge is put in place, the arbitrage provides an incremental return, with little risk. At or before the expiration of the options, the option positions are closed out. This is accomplished either by the exercise of the call, or, if the stock has dropped in price, by an exercise by the buyer of the put, in which case the stock that was sold in setting up the arbitrage position can similarly be replaced at an advantageous price. All amounts realized in closing out the arbitrage position constitute either gains or losses on the sale of stock or options, or amounts realized on the expiration of the options.

A "forward conversion" with options is a mirror image of a reverse conversion. A forward conversion involves the purchase of stocks constituting a traded Index, the purchase of a put option on such Index to hedge the long stock position, and the sale of a call option on the Index to reduce the net cost for the option hedge.

The proposed arbitrage positions are believed to be a relatively risk free method for obtaining a rate of return on the capital employed that is higher than current money market interest rates. Since the relationship between the cash prices of the relevant stock and securities and the futures contract prices, or put and call option prices, and the approximate brokers' costs and other expenses are known at the time the investment decision is made, there are relatively few circumstances that could significantly affect the expected return. The principal risks are largely avoidable, such as the failure to execute both sides of the transaction at the anticipated prices, or problems in closing out the two positions at or near the maturity of the futures or option contracts. [M] would anticipate avoiding most closing problems by timely termination of each side of the arbitrage positions somewhat in advance of the maturity of the futures or option contracts. The futures position would typically be closed by purchase or sale of an offsetting contract; where appropriate, the arbitrage position can be rolled over by purchase or sale of new futures contracts with a later maturity.

Other circumstances that might affect the expected return from the investment are not believed to have material effect in most cases, as demonstrated by substantial experience with such transactions by the firm which would be employed by [M]. Such other circumstances principally involve slight imbalances in the hedged positions, such as the possibility that the representative group of stocks (typically less than 100 percent of the stocks included in the futures Index) will not track precisely the market prices of the index. Similarly, in the case of arbitrage positions involving a long futures position in Treasury securities, unexpected variations in the market prices of the security issues that qualify for delivery could make the arbitrage position slightly unmatched, with a consequent effect on net return. Also, unanticipated dividend increases occurring during the period of a stock loan could increase the cost of borrowing the stock.

Since the proposed arbitrage positions involve relatively precise hedging, the investments therein do not involve significant exposure to stock market volatility, nor to changes in interest rates causing bond price fluctuations.

Section 511 of the Code imposes a tax on an exempt organization's unrelated business taxable income (UBTI).

Section 512(a)(1) of the Code defines UBTI in general as gross income derived by an organization from any unrelated trade or business regularly carried on by it, less the deductions that are directly connected with the carrying on of that trade or business, with certain modifications as set forth in section 512(b).

Section 512(b)(5) of the Code provides that gains or losses from the sale, exchange, or other disposition of property (other than inventory-type property) are excluded from the computation of UBTI.

Section 512(b)(4) of the Code provides that in the case of debt-financed property, certain items shall be included in or deducted from UBTI notwithstanding section 512(b)(5) and various other exclusions. Specifically, the amount ascertained under section 514(a)(1) is to be included as an item of gross income from an unrelated trade or business, and the amount ascertained under section 514(a)(2) is to be allowed as a deduction.

"Debt-financed property" is defined in relevant part by section 514(b)(1) of the Code as "any property which is held to produce income and with respect to which there is an acquisition indebtedness" at any time during the taxable year (or during the 12 months preceding disposition in the case of property disposed of during the taxable year). "Acquisition indebtedness" is defined in relevant part by section 514(c)(1) as the unpaid amount of "the indebtedness incurred by the organization in acquiring" the property and, in certain cases, indebtedness incurred before or after the acquisition. In particular, prior indebtedness is included under subsection (c)(1)(B) if it would not have been incurred but for the acquisition, and subsequent indebtedness is included under subsection (c)(1)(C) if it meets this "but for" cost [sic] and its incurrence was "reasonably foreseeable" at the time of the acquisition.

The facts submitted indicate that the investments described above by [M] would be consistent with [M]'s status as an organization described in sections 501(c)(3) and 501(f) of the Code. [M] has represented that the proposed arbitrage positions are believed to be a relatively risk free method for obtaining a rate of return higher than current money market interest rates and that the proposed arbitrage positions do not involve significant exposure to stock market volatility nor to bond price fluctuations caused by changes in interest rates.

In addition, [M] has represented that all cash or Treasury securities required for the margin accounts to support the futures contracts and for collateral security for any borrowed stock or securities would be provided from cash or securities owned by [M]. [M] has also represented that no net borrowing would at any time be made in connection with the proposed arbitrage positions. Thus, the proposed investments will not be debt-financed within the meaning of section 514(b)(1) of the Code because no acquisition indebtedness within the meaning of section 514(c)(1) of the Code will be involved. Pursuant to section 512(b)(5), therefore, gains and losses from the transactions described above will be excluded from the computation of UBTI.

Based on the information submitted we rule that:

1. Investments by [M] of its available funds in arbitrage positions involving stocks or securities and related futures or option contracts will not adversely affect [M]'s qualification as an organization described in sections 501(c)(3) and 501(f) of the Code.

2. The borrowing of stocks or securities secured by collateral of cash or Treasury securities of equivalent value; the purchase or sale of financial futures contracts, option contracts, or related stocks and securities; and the maintenance of related margin accounts will not constitute acquisition indebtedness within the meaning of section 514(c)(1) of the Code or otherwise result in unrelated business taxable income within the meaning of section 511-514 of the Code.

This ruling is based on the understanding that there will be no material changes in the facts upon which it is based.

This ruling is directed only to the organization that requested it. Section 6110(j)(3) of the Code provides that it may not be used or cited by others as precedent.

We are informing your key District Director of this action. Please keep a copy of this ruling in your permanent records.

IRS Revenue Ruling 95–8

Issue

Is the income of an exempt organization that is attributable to a short sale of publicly traded stock through a broker treated as unrelated debt-financed income within the meaning of §514 of the Internal Revenue Code and therefore subject to the unrelated business income tax under §511?

Facts

O is an organization exempt from Federal income tax under §501(a). As part of its investment strategy, O seeks to earn a profit from any decline in the value of corporation A stock, which is publicly traded. On January 2, 19yy, when the value of the stock is $5x per share, O instructs its broker to sell A stock short. To sell the stock short, O, through its broker, borrows 100 shares of A stock and sells the shares. O's broker retains the $500x sale proceeds and any income earned on these proceeds as collateral for O's obligation to return 100 shares of A stock. In addition, O puts up additional collateral of $250x cash from its own (not borrowed) funds.

The broker credits O's account with a "rebate fee," equal to a portion of the income earned on the investment of the collateral. On July 2, 19yy, the value of the stock has declined to $4x per share, and O instructs its broker to close the short sale by purchasing 100 shares of A stock for $400x and delivering the stock to the lender. O thus realizes a gain of $100x, the difference between the $500x proceeds of the sale of the borrowed stock and the $400x purchase price of the replacement stock.

Law

Section 511(a) generally imposes a tax on the "unrelated business taxable income" (UBTI) of organizations otherwise exempt from Federal income tax under §501(a) and certain other entities.

Section 513 defines the term "unrelated trade or business" as meaning in the case of an organization subject to the tax under §511, any trade or business that is not substantially related to its exempt purpose, other than through the production of income.

Section 512(a)(1) generally provides that the term "unrelated business taxable income" means the gross income derived by any organization from any unrelated trade or business, as defined in §513, regularly carried on by it, less certain deductions and subject to the modifications provided in §512(b).

Section 512(b)(1) excludes from UBTI all dividends, interest, payments with respect to certain securities loans, and annuities, and all deductions directly connected with such income.

Section 512(b)(5) excludes from UBTI gains or losses from the sale, exchange, or other disposition of property other than stock in trade or other property of a kind that would properly be included in inventory if on hand at the close of a taxable year, or property held primarily for sale to customers in the ordinary course of trade or business.

Section 512(b)(4) generally provides that notwithstanding the exclusions set out in §512(b)(1) and (b)(5), UBTI includes certain income, less deductions, derived from "debt-financed property," as defined in §514.

Section 514(b)(1) defines the term debt-financed property as any property that is held to produce income and with respect to which there is "acquisition indebtedness" at any time during the taxable year (or during the 12 months preceding disposition in the case of property disposed of during the taxable year).

Section 514(c)(1) provides that the term acquisition indebtedness means, with respect to any debt-financed property, the unpaid amount of (A) indebtedness incurred by the organization in acquiring or improving the property, (B) indebtedness incurred before the acquisition or improvement of the property if the indebtedness would not have been incurred but for the acquisition or improvement, and (C) indebtedness incurred after the acquisition or improvement of the property if the indebtedness would not have been incurred but for the acquisition or improvement and the incurrence of the indebtedness was reasonably foreseeable at the time of the acquisition or improvement.

Analysis

Income attributable to a short sale can be income derived from debt-financed property only if the short seller incurs acquisition indebtedness within the meaning of §514 with respect to the property on which the short seller realizes that income. In *Deputy v. du Pont,* 308 US 488, 497–98 (1940), 1940–1 CB 118, 122, the Supreme Court held that although a short sale created an obligation, it did not create indebtedness for purposes of the predecessor of §163. Therefore, neither the $100x gain realized by O on the short sale attributable to the decline in value of A stock from $5x to $4x nor income derived from the proceeds of the short sale, such as the rebate fee earned by O, is income from debt-financed property within the meaning of §514.

Holding

If an exempt organization sells publicly traded stock short through a broker, then neither the gain or loss attributable to the change in value of the underlying stock nor the rebate fee is income or loss derived from debt-financed property within the meaning of §514. No inference is intended with respect to a borrowing of property other than publicly traded stock sold short through a broker.

Drafting Information
The principal author of this revenue ruling is Charles Barrett of the Exempt Organizations Division of the Office of the Assistant Commissioner (Employee Plans/Exempt Organizations). For further information regarding this revenue ruling, contact Mr. Barrett on (202) 622-8152.

3

⑥ STRUCTURE IMPLICATIONS OF MARKET NEUTRAL: A NEW PERSPECTIVE ON ACTIVE MANAGEMENT

Robert E. Shultz

The management of pension, endowment, and other large institutional asset pools can be traced from the passage of ERISA[1] in 1974. The principal focus here is on the inherent problems with the multiple-manager structure and the steps taken over the years to cope with its recognized deficiencies. The solutions to these problems and their effectiveness are examined from the author's perspective.

From this background, an industry structure based on market-neutral portfolio construction techniques will be put forth as the most efficient solution to date for the multiple-manager dilemma.

Of equal importance to the question of "can active management add value" is whether the normal multiple-manager environment permits (1) the proper attribution of

The author wishes to express his appreciation to William E. Jacques, Hal L. Arbit, Sue R. Davenport, and John C. Winchester for their invaluable contributions. Particular thanks go to Bill Jacques for putting up with all of the brainstorming telephone conversations, and for permitting the use of concepts developed by Martingale Asset Management.
1. Employee Retirement Income Security Act of 1974.

return, and (2) the flow of value added to the fund's bottom line total return.[2]

EVOLUTION OF INSTITUTIONAL INVESTING
Advent of ERISA

To gain an understanding of the issues, it is necessary to begin with the passage of ERISA in September 1974. Those managing pension funds and their first cousins, endowments and foundations, remember the language of the act as being very scary. The message was wrapped in terms of "prudent man," "diversification," and "avoidance of large losses." Fund fiduciaries, whose personal financial benefit from risk taking was little or none, need not have been lectured on the likely outcome of maverick risk[3] in this environment.

Focus of Diversification

Most funds at the time were managed by one institution, likely the trust department of the organization's lead commercial bank. Diversification concerns led many sponsors to add additional balanced managers. From this point, the era of specialization took hold with a vengeance, and with it the magnification of the deficiencies of the multiple-manager structure. The various stages of specialization were

- Single balanced
- Multiple balanced
- Asset class specialists
- Style within asset class
- Capitalization specialists

2. For those who have lived through the era and wish to bypass the evolution of the multiple-manager dilemma, page 46 begins the section on market neutral as the solution.
3. Maverick risk is a term used many years later to describe pursuing strategies different from the consensus.

MULTIPLE-MANAGER DEFICIENCIES

A well-worn list, by no means exhaustive, of the potential deficiencies inherent in multiple-manager structures includes

- Dissipation of best decisions
- Overdiversification with high fees
- Lack of risk control
- "Closet" indexing
- Growth (creates need for many managers)
- Managers' business risk (overrules investment risk)

One of the earlier spokesmen on the subject was Barr Rosenberg, founder of BARRA, who appeared on the cover of the May 1978, issue of *Institutional Investor* with the apt question, "Who is Barr Rosenberg and what the hell is he talking about?"

Let's look back at Barr Rosenberg, circa 1978, when he presented Berkeley Working Paper 65, "Institutional Investment with Multiple-Portfolio Managers," at the *Institutional Investor* Spring Roundtable. Barr made the following four key observations:

- "The institutional investment arrangement of multiple-portfolio managers is too often taken for granted."
- "The use of autonomous multiple managers implies a system for decentralized decision making."
- "If money is left with managers, will the sum of the portfolio be as efficient as building one portfolio?"
- "In the long run, if multiple-management systems are not reconstituted, there will be a tendency toward multiple-advisor systems."

On the first point one might comment, Well, that may be true, but what are the implications? Are they bad? On the second, we should focus on the word implies. At that time, and for that matter today, the models used to ensure that the total actions represent the efficient linking of independent actions are flawed at best, and at worst not used by plan sponsors.

The third point can be viewed by reference to the Law of Optimality, which simply states that it is at least as good to optimize one's whole problem as it is to optimize subsets of the problem. In other words, if all managers optimize their portions of the assets, the sponsor's aggregate portfolio may not be optimal.

Barr concluded with the bold pronouncement that if the deficiencies were not addressed, the industry would move toward a multiple-advisor structure. Simply put, the plan sponsor would purchase "insights" (such as analysts' recommendations or buy/sell lists) from multiple-investment firms and construct an optimal portfolio "in house," thereby acquiescing to the Law of Optimality.

Before leaving the 1978 Spring Roundtable, let's conclude with Barr's issues in multiple management, delivered in a parental tone, and use the list as a backdrop in assessing plan-sponsor actions over the period:

A. Multiple management can at best match optimal practice in a centralized portfolio with multiple advisors.

B. Whether there are one or many managers, the return on the aggregate portfolio is what matters to the sponsor.

C. Aggregated normal holdings should coincide with the sponsor's target portfolio.

D. Aggressiveness should vary inversely with the manager's investment proportion.

E. Investment aggressiveness should vary in response to the sponsor's assessment of the manager's ability.

F. The desired aggressiveness for each manager is influenced by the correlation between his or her information process and that of the other managers.

    G. Never pay an active management fee for passive management.

    H. Use passive management to reduce residual risk.

    I. Multiple active managers are not a means to reduce risk, but rather a means to obtain superior reward.

    J. Multiple active managers should be compared to a single active manager.

The pronouncements of Rosenberg convey an important message. While few would take exception to any points on the list of issues, we may need a reminder of their importance from time to time. As David Tierney of the consulting firm Richards & Tierney puts it, "I am continually amazed that many plan sponsors spend 90 percent of their time on the stock, asset, and portfolio level and 10 percent on macro fund structure issues, rather than the reverse." I contend that success on the micro level is often swamped by inattentiveness to the macro issues.[4]

INDEX MANAGEMENT

From the stock selection focus of the early 1970s, plan sponsors in the mid-70s began to fix on indexing as a solution to the multiple-manager dilemma.[5] The trend was directly linked to the increasing numbers and rising influence of those trained in the school of modern portfolio theory.

---

4. The author numbers himself among the plan sponsors and in no way holds himself outside any critical comments on actions of sponsors.
5. The author vividly recalls presenting to the Pension Committee of the Board in 1974 the recommendation to index a sizable share of New York Telephone's equity portfolio. At the conclusion of the presentation, the chairman and others said this was so new to them that they felt committee member Gus Levy (deceased, former chairman of Goldman Sachs) should make the decision. After tipping back his chair and puffing on a cigar for what seemed like an eternity, he said, "It was a good idea," and the committee should approve. Savvy Wall Street person that he was, rather than lament the decreased trading resulting from indexing, he positioned Goldman Sachs as the leading trader of index portfolios.

Indexing, or, more properly, passive management, ad-dressed many of the issues raised by Rosenberg and had the most pervasive impact on institutional asset management of any strategy over the period. After overcoming the hurdle that indexing was a much deeper issue than the early de-bates about accepting mediocrity implied, the 1980s wit-nessed an explosive growth of passive management.

ACTIVE–PASSIVE STRUCTURE

Hal Arbit[6] of American National Bank, Chicago, first ap-plied the concept of core/noncore, or active–passive as it came to be known, to the notion that sponsors should pas-sively manage their core portfolio and seek active man-agers for value added from active insights.[7]

A statement often made was that plan sponsors should passively manage all assets in the portfolio for which active managers with demonstrated skill in alpha generation were not available. I equate activeness to the willingness of the manager to depart from holding a market or bench-mark portfolio. These departures are commonly reflected in the number of issues held, but can also be measured by sec-tor or industry concentration as well as exposure to a par-ticular factor or factors.

Based on the "willingness to depart" definition of "ac-tive," I developed the following criteria for selecting active managers:

- Best investors (exclusive of style)
- Willing to make and comfortable making major bets

---

6. Although Barr Rosenberg became the one-name celebrity like Cher, Hal Arbit, then at American National Bank in Chicago, could lay claim to having been the one responsible. His early commitment went to the extent of mortgag-ing his house and sending Barr the proceeds when a contractual dispute at the bank resulted in the delay of the second installment to fund the project that was the beginning of Barra.
7. American National Bank sponsored a seminar in 1975 titled "A New Look at Investment Strategy," and another titled "Active–Passive" in May of 1978.

- Stable organizations (already done all their moving)
- Sound business plan to manage growth
- Strategy capable of absorbing significant assets
- Insights of value to total fund

DIVERSIFIED ACTIVE MANAGEMENT

The 1990s have witnessed a focus on diversified active management with *meaningful* use of passive management. Although the blend of active and passive portfolio construction techniques could have provided a solution to many of the issues of "multiple-manager mush,"[8] the approach did not accomplish the desired objective. The principal hindrance was the lack of any meaningful change in the actively managed portion of the assets. As Hal Arbit recollects, "Most sponsors viewed index funds as a hedge on their active managers rather than an approach which allowed them to exploit active management." Two often-seen charts support the point. Figure 3–1 shows that a sponsor with five managers has little likelihood of adding significant return over the market, since 95 percent of variance (return potential) comes from the market itself.[9]

Figure 3–2 supports the conclusion reached by Hal Arbit and Barr Rosenberg in 1973 that the vast majority of multiply-managed portfolios do not reflect the intent or expectations of the plan sponsor.[10] The choice of market return and standard deviation are not important and the reader should feel free to substitute at will. By investing in the S&P 500 Index, one must assume a risk tolerance of one percent return for bearing 66.7 units of variance.

---

8. Multiple-manager mush is the author's term for the deficiencies of multiply-managed portfolios.
9. The author acknowledges that the linkage between variance and return is a complex issue.
10. Barr Rosenberg and Hal Arbit, "Portfolio Management from the Sponsor Viewpoint," unpublished, 1973.

FIGURE 3-1

Components of Variance

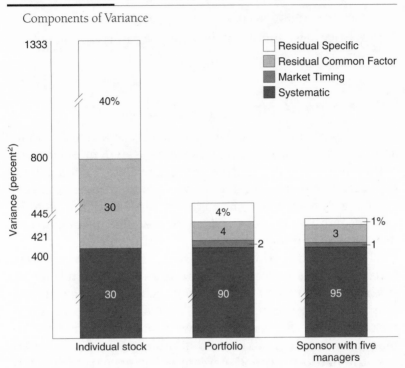

Source: Barra.

Applying that same trade-off to the residual standard deviation of the average active portfolio implies an expectation of only 38 basis points from active management. Large numbers of active managers only exacerbate the void between expectation and reality, in that the 38 basis points would be further reduced.

This risk–return trade-off implies that plan sponsors have a lower tolerance for accepting residual risk than systematic (market) risk.

Another explanation, and an old saw, is that the managers' awareness of business risk so dominates their outlook on investment risk that no amount of direction will lead them to construct portfolios that deliver risk–return

FIGURE 3–2

Required Alpha

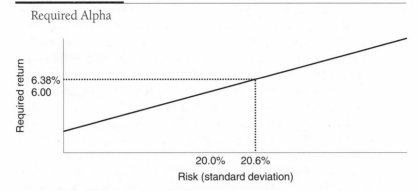

S&P 500: Mean return 6%   Standard deviation 20% = 400 units of variance; 400/6 = 66.7 units of variance for 1% return

Managed Portfolio: Residual standard deviation 5% = 25 units of variance; 25/66.7 = 0.38%

Source: Barra.

trade-offs that meet the client's expectations, given a mix of active and passive management. The answer, I suspect, lies somewhere in the middle. Certainly there has been no lengthy list of sponsors who have championed increased aggressiveness by their managers.

MULTIPLE INSIGHTS VERSUS MULTIPLE MANAGERS

If the reader can accept for the moment that most of the deficiencies cited in the multiple-manager process persist and that few overt actions have been instituted, let's examine the business in multiple-insight structure. The key to the multiple-insight structure is information. What information? From where in the investment manager's process? These critical issues are discussed in the following excerpt from a letter from Bill Jacques:[11]

---

11. Letter from William E. Jacques, chief investment officer, Martingale Asset Management, to Robert E. Shultz, September 1, 1988.

Information: What information do you want from the manager? Do you want the trading list, the actual buys or sells? Or, do you want the insights themselves, what we quants call the alphas? If the managers can quantify their process, then you clearly want the alphas, since the trading list combines the pure insights with portfolio construction rules (that may be inappropriate for the aggregate portfolio). If the managers cannot quantify their process, then the trading list is the best you can do. [However, in a world of real-time valuation models, what those who use information contained in every transaction want (remember every trade gives you some information about what someone thinks a company is worth) is an on-line version of the manager's valuation model. Good luck getting that!]

Trading: From the plan sponsor's point of view, centralized trading residing with the plan sponsor makes the most sense. You will capture the economies of scale of lower commissions and avoid offsetting trades. However, from the managers' point of view, they like to trade all accounts in a coordinated fashion. You may be bumping up against them in the market and screwing up their orders. Or maybe, if you're quick on the trigger, do a little front running. Finally, the managers would fight to the bitter end since they lose the flow of soft dollars, which are more important to investment managers than men to Madonna.

Performance: How do you measure the performance of your managers? Is it the I.C. (information coefficient) of the manager's alpha, or is it how well their other accounts performed? What if your use of the manager's insights has a larger payoff than the manager's use of his insights—do you split the difference?

Fees: Are managers compensated on the basis of how well the whole fund does or their specific contribution? What is their specific contribution? How much money are they "managing" for you?

Trust: How do you assure that the insights the managers give you are their best insights? Do they trust you? You could be using the insights for a far larger portion of your total portfolio than the firm is being compensated for.

FIGURE 3–3

The Ongoing Evolution of Institutional Investment Management

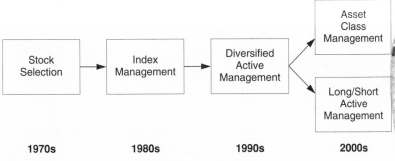

Source: John D. Freeman, Vice President, Martingale Asset Management.

- Exposure to an asset class and capturing active insights are totally unrelated processes.
- Any active portfolio equals an index or benchmark portfolio plus a long/short portfolio.
- The correct solution is a passive exposure to the asset class combined with insight-efficient long/short portfolios.
- Multiple-manager structure exacerbates the problems of traditional active management.

Let's examine each of these statements and introduce the deadweight[14] concept, which is a measure of the degree to which an active portfolio is actually passively managed. It is akin to the negative connotation of "closet indexing." Deadweight is defined as the lesser of the benchmark weight or the holdings for all assets in the portfolio.

---

14. The term and concept are attributable to Martingale Asset Management. For those interested in further discussion of the deadweight issue, see the forthcoming paper by John D. Freeman and William E. Jacques.

There are three forms of deadweight in long-only space:

1. Stocks held at the benchmark weight (a) produce passive returns, (b) use capital, and (c) are subject to active fees.

2. Stocks overweighted compared to the benchmark (a) use capital to bring them to benchmark weight, and (b) are subject to active fees at benchmark weight.

3. Stocks underweighted compared to the benchmark contribute to active returns only if they underperform the benchmark.

Viewing assets as the capital of the portfolio, stocks held at the benchmark weight consume capital and produce only passive returns. In the case of overweighting, capital used to bring the issue to the benchmark weight wastes capital in that only the passive benchmark return is earned on the benchmark weighting. Stocks underweighted relative to the benchmark provide positive active return only if the issue underperforms the benchmark. Thereby none of the capital used for an underweighted position contributes to value added.

Estimates of typical levels of deadweight in an active portfolio range from 50 to 75 percent.[15] This percent can rise dramatically when holdings of multiple-manager portfolios are aggregated at the fund level. Since the percentage of deadweight equates to the proportion to be passively managed, the passive portion is assumed to be in the 80 to 90 percent range.

Another perverse observation is that the better benchmarks created by the normal portfolio construction process only serve to magnify the deadweight proportion. One of the tests applied by a leading consultant to determine the

---

15. Estimates by Martingale Asset Management.

quality of the benchmark is benchmark coverage, that is, the proportion of the actual portfolio's market value contained in the benchmark.[16]

If these statements are taken to heart, active managers should be permitted to sell short; the proper benchmark should be a cash return plus some residual risk premium; and there should be no deadweight, with futures and passive strategies used to gain asset class exposure.

Would that the world were so simple! Obviously a number of significant issues remain to be addressed before we consider the "world after deadweight." But first, an observation on the term "market neutral." Market neutral is not an asset class but a portfolio construction technique. Although a constraint-free cash benchmark (plus a risk premium) is a proper standard against which return and residual risk should be measured, market neutral should not be confused with or referred to as enhanced cash management.

Next, market-neutral returns derive from active equity management and can produce large negative residual returns. Any investment organization that lacks skill in managing long-only portfolios will magnify its shortcomings in managing long/short portfolios. Construction techniques do not improve insights! Even managers who have a demonstrated record of adding value in long-only portfolios may not be successful with long/short strategies, as shorting requires a different decision process.

Third, but vitally significant, is the overlapping universe problem. Without solution, this will be at least of the magnitude present in long-only multiple-manager funds. Paul Fullum, when he worked at the IBM Retirement Fund in 1982, proposed, in jest, a solution that is elegant in its simplicity. He would assign Manager 1 with stocks beginning with "A" through "C"; Manager 2 with stocks "D" through "F"; and so on.

---

16. Jeffrey V. Bailey, "Evaluating Benchmark Quality," *Financial Analysts Journal*, May/June 1992, pp 33–39.

William Gurner, formerly the plan sponsor at Federal Express and currently president of an investment management firm, believes the solution to the problem of overlap may be industry sector assignments. To date he has focused only on long portfolios. It would appear logical that knowing more about less should be superior to knowing less about more, particularly in the absence of index constraints.

THE WORLD AFTER DEADWEIGHT

Examination of some of the implications of the new perspective reveal the following shifts in focus:

Absolute versus Relative Returns   The focus of plan sponsors and investment managers would turn to absolute as opposed to the relative return standard present in the current structure.

Low Correlations versus High Correlations   Removal of deadweight and solution of the overlapping universes should lead to lower correlations across active managers and strategies.

Liquidity Providers versus Liquidity Demanders   As an array of market-neutral managers would contain a significant representation of arbitrage strategies, there would be a natural growth in liquidity-supplying trades as opposed to liquidity-demanding trades.

Virtual Reality   With our virtual-reality glasses firmly in place, other observations become readily apparent concerning the impact of the new structure:

- *Performance Attribution*. The separation of systematic risk from residual return greatly simplifies the attribution process and removes the "smoke, mystique, and mirrors"[17] that have plagued sponsors trying to answer the question, Have my active managers added value? Manager meetings would focus solely on how the manager performed and would not become involved in how the market performed.

- *Identification of Skill.* While still a difficult task, sponsor identification of managers with valuable insights would be more straightforward. While the issue of the proper time horizon over which to measure skill would not disappear, it would be shortened. The universe of managers would undergo a significant winnowing process.

- *Costs.* Fees for the passive portion of the assets would obviously be greatly reduced. However, the picture becomes a bit unclear as to active management fees. Logically, the fees would increase since the sponsor would be purchasing pure insight rather than a combination of asset class exposure and active insights. One view suggests that, given an 80-percent passive component and 20-percent active (market neutral) component, fees could increase up to five times their current levels for those managers with top-quartile skill levels.

- *Trading Volumes.* Here the glasses are clear, but the picture is not an intuitive one. At first glance one can envision volumes dropping significantly, as trading for the passive portion (except rebalancing required for index changes) would result only on a one-time basis for flows in or out of the asset class. However, we must think in long/short space rather than long only. The following example illustrates

---

17. "Smoke, mystique, and mirrors" is a term used by the author over the years to describe the performance measurement process.

that ongoing trading volume would remain
unchanged under the new structure.

	IBM			GE		
	Index Portion	Active Weight	Weight	Index Portion	Active Weight	Weight
Current	3%	2%	1%	0%	2%	(2%)
Sell	3	—	—			
Buy				3	2	1

In long/short space, 3 percent of IBM must be sold
to reduce the active weight to zero and, conversely,
an active 1-percent position in GE requires a
3-percent purchase since by holding no GE the
effective position was a 2-percent underweighting.

CONCLUSION

While a fair amount of this chapter discussion has been
conceptual, the multiple-manager dilemma is real, and
needs additional focus from the managers of institutional
pools of assets.

ⓢ ## ARE LONG/SHORT EQUITY STRATEGIES SUPERIOR?

Richard O. Michaud, Ph.D.
Senior Vice President
Acadian Asset Management

Suppose you have a reliable forecast of the performance of a universe of stocks. Traditionally you would use the information to buy or "go long" a portfolio of undervalued stocks. Proponents of a long-short strategy argue that there is valuable information in the forecast that is not being used. They claim that a long/short portfolio consisting of long positions in undervalued stocks (a "long" portfolio) and short positions in an equal value portfolio of overvalued stocks (a "short" portfolio), where market risk is minimized ("market-neutral"), can achieve twice the expected active return of the traditional long-only portfolio with minimal risk.

This chapter demonstrates that claims of the superiority of long-short investing often reflect misunderstanding of basic concepts of modern investment management and may result in unrealistic expectations. Analysis of portfolio risk reveals that the increases in expected return gained by long/short investing are generally accompanied by comparable increases in risk. Additionally, the active risk level of long/short strategies is often substantially greater than normal active management and may be incompatible with the objectives of many long-term institutional investors.

The argument ignores some practical considerations, such as increased trading costs and the likelihood of large losses, that can have a significant negative effect on the performance of long/short portfolios. The discussion focuses on comparing long with long/short active equity strategies and does not directly consider the issues raised in a multi-manager context.

LEVERAGE OR RESTRICTED BORROWING

In a long/short strategy, the investor can use the income received from selling short to buy securities. Ignoring transaction costs, the strategy can be self-financing and require no investment. In practice, the investor establishes an account with a broker that requires cash or other securities. Financial frictions limit the level of self-financing. Roughly, a $100 dollar investment allows the purchase and sale of $100 in long and short portfolios plus a $100 investment in a low-risk cash asset.[1] This implies that a long/short strategy is roughly a two-for-one leveraging, or restricted borrowing, process that transforms a $100 investment into two $100 equity portfolios. Because the strategy results in two portfolios, it is often described as a "two alpha" strategy.

Measuring Value Added

As with any active equity strategy, the proper measure of the value added by an active long/short equity portfolio is the amount of residual (active) risk compared with the

---

1. Currently, the actual amount is closer to a $95 investment in the long and short portfolios. However, $100 is convenient for explanatory purposes. This assumption tilts the argument in favor of long/short strategies. The difference between $100 and the actual amount of the investment leads to an additional fixed cost associated with long/short investing.

residual (active) return, both measured with respect to an appropriate benchmark. The level of systematic risk is often irrelevant.[2]

In order to reduce risk, long/short managers often construct hedged or market-neutral portfolios, which are structured to have minimal market risk. The theoretical absence of systematic risk changes how value added is measured. The residual return in this case is measured with respect to the strategy's cash rate, which is similar to the T-bill rate, instead of the return on an equity index. This is because the minimum active risk position of a market-neutral long/short manager is not investment in an equity index but the absence of investment in equities.[3]

Because there are relatively few long/short equity managers, their relative performances may not be very reliable. A simple alternative is to measure performance by "equitizing," or adding the return of an appropriate equity index to the residual return generated by the long/short portfolio. This allows comparisons of relative performance across the spectrum of active equity managers.

Unfilled Expectations

A market-neutral long/short portfolio is a hybrid investment strategy: In some ways it resembles normal active equity management, in others, fixed-income management. Its paradoxical characteristics can be the source of

---

2. The notion of measuring the active risk and return of a short portfolio may not be obvious. Consider the following related question: Does a short index portfolio have any active risk or return? Upon reflection, a short index can have no active risk or return. Consequently, active risk and return in a short portfolio must be measured with respect to negative index-weights. Multiplying portfolio weights and index weights by minus one reduces the analysis of a short portfolio's risk and return to the usual long-portfolio problem.

3. More precisely, the efficient zero-residual-risk market-neutral long/short strategy is long the index minus (short) the index plus cash. The long and short index-positions cancel so that the position is equivalent to no position in equities.

contradictory claims by managers and unfulfilled expectations for owners of the assets.

A long/short strategy is active equity investment. Capital is invested in equities and the value-added risk and return is active equity risk and return. However, the strategy also resembles cash management. This is because portfolio return is designed to exceed a cash rate, not the return on an equity index. Consequently, an unsophisticated investor may assume that a long/short portfolio provides active equity returns with fixed-income risk. If so, disappointment is likely.

Short Selling and Long Portfolios

Some managers claim that only long/short strategies both sell overvalued stocks and buy undervalued stocks.[4] Such a statement reflects a serious misunderstanding of basic principles of modern asset management.

Active portfolio risk is defined with respect to overweightings and underweightings relative to index weights. No matter how risk is measured, the index has zero active risk. If the benchmark is the S&P 500, a 50-stock long portfolio is "short" the 450 index stocks not included in the portfolio. Not only long/short strategies but all active strategies are "two alpha" portfolios.[5]

Note that many active managers do not ignore sell information. Modern asset managers assign negative alphas to overvalued stocks and optimization procedures typically lead to underweightings. If some conventional asset managers improperly neglect sell decisions, any inefficiency created is exploitable by many long as well as long/short managers. As many large institutions use modern asset management techniques, it would be surprising if sell information inefficiencies are persistent and economically significant.

---

4. See S. Hansell, "The Other Side of Zero," *Institutional Investor,* April 1992.
5. This is a term used in Hansell to describe the allegedly unique but erroneous "two alpha" character of long/short portfolios.

In terms of active risk and return, a long portfolio can be described as an "unleveraged long/short strategy." As efficient long portfolios use sell as well as buy information efficiently, the relevant question is: Except for leverage, what's different about long/short portfolios?

LONG/SHORT STRATEGY RETURNS

By definition, a long/short strategy results in two fully invested portfolios. The return is the difference between the long and short (before shorting) portfolios. Define R_{LS} as the excess (above the riskless rate) return of the long/short portfolio:

$$R_{LS} = R_L - R_S \tag{1}$$

where R_L and R_S denote the excess return of the long and short portfolios.

In a long/short strategy, the long and short portfolios can be managed separately. The result is that a long/short strategy may be "less index-constrained" than a long-only portfolio; that is, sell information may be reflected in larger underweightings with respect to index weights than in a long-only portfolio. Consequently, a long/short portfolio may enhance the impact of forecast information.[6]

---

6. Consider the following simple example. A stock index consists of two stocks with the following index weights and alphas: $i_1 = 0.8$, $i_2 = 0.2$, $\alpha_1 = 2\%$, $\alpha2 = -8\%$. Buy stock one is the maximum alpha long portfolio and

$$\alpha_L = 2\% \ [0.2 \times 2 + (-0.2 \times -8)].$$

Sell stock two is the maximum alpha short portfolio and

$$\alpha_S = 8\% \ [-(-0.8 \times 2) + 0.8 \times -8].$$

The long/short strategy alpha is 10%, which is much more than two times the maximum long-portfolio alpha. Long/short investing may improve the reward-risk ratio because it may be "less index-constrained" when reflecting sell information.

Assume that the excess return of security i, r_i, is consistent with the security market line of the capital asset pricing model:[7]

$$r_i = \beta_i R_m + \varepsilon_i \qquad (2)$$

where

β_i = beta of stock i,
R_m = market excess return, and
ε_i = residual return of security i.

Let

R_P = portfolio P excess return,
ε_P = portfolio P residual return,
β_P = portfolio systematic risk, and
ω_P^2 = $V(\varepsilon_P)$ = portfolio residual risk.

Let α_L and α_S represent the after shorting expected residual (systematic risk adjusted) excess return or "alpha" of R_L and R_S. Then:

$$\alpha_L + \alpha_S = E(\varepsilon_L - \varepsilon_S). \qquad (3)$$

Assuming that the forecasting power is symmetric for the top and bottom ranked stocks, then $\alpha_L = \alpha_S$ and:[8]

$$\alpha_{LS} = 2\alpha_L. \qquad (4)$$

That is, the long/short strategy has twice the long-portfolio alpha.

---

7. See W. F. Sharpe "Capital Asset Prices: A Theory of Market Equilibrium under Conditions of Risk," *Journal of Finance,* September 1964, and J. Lintner, "The Valuation of Risk Assets and the Selection of Risky Investments in Stock Portfolios and Capital Budgets," *Review of Economics and Statistics,* February 1965. The argument does not depend on the validity of any particular model of risk, only that the dichotomy of systematic and residual risk holds.

8. As footnote 6 makes clear, the long and short portfolio alphas need not be equal. However, this assumption is convenient for pedagogical purposes.

Long/Short Strategy Risk

From Equation (2), the total risk (variance) of a long/short portfolio is:

$$V_{LS} = V\{(\beta_L - \beta_S)R_m + \varepsilon_L - \varepsilon_S\}. \tag{5}$$

Assuming that the long/short portfolio is hedged against market risk and the long and short portfolios have similar risk characteristics, then $\beta_L = \beta_S$, $\omega_{L^2} = \omega_S^2$ and:

$$V_{LS} = \omega^2_{LS} = 2\omega_L^2\{1 + \rho\}, \tag{6}$$

where ρ is the correlation of the long- and (after-shorting) short-portfolio alphas. To simplify further, if the long- and short-portfolio alphas are uncorrelated, then:

$$\omega^2_{LS} = 2\omega_L^2. \tag{7}$$

Do these results imply that the strategy is an economic free lunch? While total risk may decrease, Equations (6) and (7) indicate that increases in active return are typically accompanied by increases in active risk. The question is not whether residual risk is increased by a long/short strategy, but by how much.

Some preliminary data is available for comparing the active risk of long-only strategies with long/short portfolios. Under current market conditions (see the Appendix), the residual standard deviation of a typical institutional, normal active, long-only portfolio can be estimated as 3.5 percent. Current estimates of the risk of market-neutral long/short portfolios are in the range of 5 percent to 15 percent.[9] This indicates that the active risk multiplier for long/short strategies is on the order of three. At the upper range, market-neutral long/short strategies may be nearly as risky as the market. One important implication is that risk adjustment

9. Estimates by N. Ramachandran, "Using Market-Neutral Strategies to Add Value to Your Portfolio." *Market-Neutral (Long-Short) Investment Strategies Conference,* Institute for International Research, New York, November 1992.

is essential when comparing the performance of long/short strategies with that of long-only strategies.

Portfolio Gammas

Is the increase in expected active return associated with a long/short strategy advantageous given the increase in active risk? A natural way of comparing the relative benefits of investment strategies is to compare ratios of expected active return to active risk.

Define the portfolio's gamma, Γ, as the ratio of active return to risk:

$$\Gamma = \alpha/\omega. \tag{8}$$

Under the assumptions in Equations (4) and (6), the ratio of the gamma of a long/short strategy relative to the gamma of the long-only portfolio is:

$$\Gamma_{LS}/\Gamma_L = \sqrt{2(1+\rho)}. \tag{9}$$

Equation (9) shows that a long/short strategy improves the active risk-return characteristics of a long portfolio whenever $\rho < 1$. This result can be cited as a rationale for the superiority of long/short strategies.

Unfortunately, long- and short-portfolio alphas may be highly positively correlated in practice. A long/short strategy is generally designed to extract more active return from a "best forecast" set of alphas.[10] In this case, the alphas used to structure the long and short portfolios are the same. Consequently, the value of ρ depends on differences in portfolio active weights that are likely to be the same in

---

10. Anecdotal evidence indicates that some long/short managers claim to use different valuation processes for long and short portfolios in order to reduce the value of ρ. Such a process, if it exists, may have dubious investment value. Whether or not a stock is part of a long or short portfolio would appear to be independent of whether it is over- or undervalued.

sign and similar in magnitude.[11] As a result, a long/short strategy may not substantially improve upon the investment characteristics of a long portfolio.

A key to potential benefits is whether and when ρ is significantly less than one. Because Γ ratio analysis does not hold the level of active risk constant, proper comparisons of long and long/short strategies require efficient frontier analysis.

EFFICIENT FRONTIERS

Consider the residual-risk/return efficient frontier for long/short strategies illustrated in Figure 4–1. The origin, labeled "(long) index—(short) index," is an efficient market-neutral, long/short portfolio with zero active risk. The efficient frontier is labeled "Long/Short" and extends upward from the origin. The long-only residual risk-return efficient frontier, labeled "Long," curves upward from the origin. Shading indicates where the long and long/short efficient frontiers differ. The efficient zero residual-risk/return long-only portfolio is the index.

The long-only efficient frontier is dominated by the long/short efficient frontier in the sense that, at any given level of residual risk, the long/short efficient frontier will never have less alpha, or a smaller gamma, than the long efficient frontier. In investment terms, long/short portfolios are never more index-constrained than long-only portfolios.

---

11. To see this, let w^L and w^S denote the active weights in the long and short optimal portfolios. Then, by definition,

$$\alpha_L = \Sigma \mathrm{w}_i^L \times \alpha_i \text{ and}$$

$$\alpha_S = -(\Sigma w_i^S \times \alpha_i) = \Sigma w_i^S \times -\alpha_i = \Sigma(-w_i^S)\alpha_i.$$

As footnote 6 illustrates, w_i^L and $-w_i^S$ have the same sign. More generally, since w_i^L and w_i^S will tend to have the same sign as α_i and $-\alpha_i$ respectively, after shorting w_i^L and $-w_i^S$ will tend to have the same sign for each security. In many practical cases, the magnitudes will often be similar. Consequently, the correlation of α_L and α_S is likely to be positive and large. Intuitively, the short portfolio does not alter the overweighting (underweighting) of positive (negative) alpha stocks, but it may allow larger active weights than the long portfolio.

FIGURE 4–1

Residual-Risk/Return Efficient Frontiers for Long/Short and Long
Portfolios

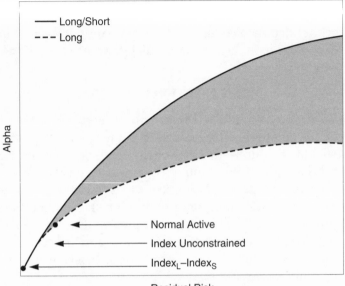

Under reasonable conditions, however, the long/short
efficient frontier coincides with the long-only efficient frontier at and near the origin, i.e., for low-residual-risk portfolios.[12] This result is shown in Figure 4–1 where the long
and market-neutral long/short efficient frontiers coincide

---

12. The condition that all stocks are in the index and have non-zero positive index
weights is sufficient, by continuity, to guarantee the existence of index-unconstrained efficient long/short portfolios at sufficiently low levels of residual risk. This means that the two efficient frontiers coincide at and near
the origin. To see this, equitize the market-neutral long/short portfolio by
adding an index fund. The residual risk-return of the equitized portfolio is
the same as that of the market-neutral long/short portfolio. At zero residual risk, the efficient equitized market-neutral long/short portfolio is not
index-constrained, it is simply the index. Consequently, the residual mean
and variance can be replicated by a long-only efficient portfolio, namely an
index fund. By continuity, for sufficiently low levels of residual

in a region that includes the origin. It is only when long efficient portfolios are index-constrained that the two efficient frontiers deviate.[13]

Let *NA* represent a long-only efficient portfolio with a level of residual risk typical of institutional "normal active" risk-controlled portfolios. Assume that the forecasting process is not pathological or inefficient and that *NA* is near the long/short efficient frontier.

Fixed Costs and Efficiency

Consider the effect of including the additional costs often associated with managing long/short portfolios.[14] As Figure 4–2 shows, when additional fixed costs are included, the long/short efficient frontier shifts downward by a constant amount. The long/short efficient frontier now consists of two segments—the long-only efficient frontier at low levels of residual risk and the long/short-plus-fixed-costs efficient frontier at higher levels of residual risk. This is shown in Figure 4–2 with shading below the curve for parts of the frontier that are efficient. Note that typical long-only efficient institutional portfolios, as represented by *NA*, may be long/short efficient. The results indicate that long-only portfolios are preferable at low levels of residual risk, while

risk (small neighborhood of the origin), the equitized market-neutral long/short efficient-frontier portfolios are not index-constrained. Consequently, their (combined) active weights can be replicated exactly by a long-only portfolio. As long-only portfolios can't be more efficient than index-unconstrained long-short portfolios, the efficient frontiers are the same.

13. Note the consistency of this result with the observations made earlier on the gamma ratio of long/short portfolios.

14. Long/short strategies may have a number of fixed, as well as variable, costs not normally associated with long-only asset management. One fixed cost is that operating cash must be set aside for day-to-day management of the short portfolio. Also, long/short managers generally have increased infrastructure costs associated with the need to manage twice as many portfolios per $100 under management, as well as specialized procedures for managing short portfolios. The net impact of fixed costs, which is likely to be reflected in increased management fees, is dependent, in part, on the level of assets under management.

FIGURE 4–2

Residual Risk/Return Efficient Frontiers for Long/Short Portfolios with Fixed Costs

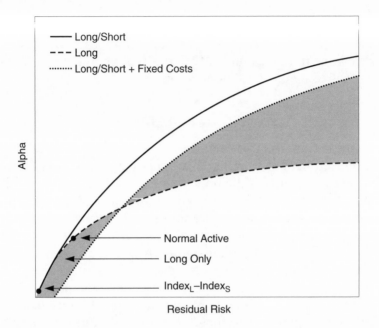

long/short strategies are preferable at higher levels of residual risk.[15] Figure 4–2 indicates that, depending on the level of additional costs, even fairly risky efficient long-only portfolios may be long/short efficient.

Without further assumptions, long/short strategies are not inherently more efficient or superior to long-only portfolios. They are simply part of the continuum of active investment strategies. They represent an extension of the

15. The analysis in Figure 4–2 does not consider the option of placing a portion of a $100 investment in a long portfolio and the remainder in a long/short strategy. The net effect of varying the proportion of a $100 investment in a long/short strategy relative to a long-only portfolio may be to "fill in" the efficient frontier in Figure 4–2. (I am indebted to V. D'Silva for this observation). While of interest, the issue is essentially related to the multimanager context and is beyond the scope of the paper.

investment-opportunity set that may increase after-fixed-costs gamma at above-normal levels of active risk.

MARKET NEUTRALITY AND OPTIMIZATION

In the context of the long/short strategy, market risk is uncompensated, hence reduces the attractiveness of the strategy. However, market neutrality is not easy to achieve; few portfolios are truly market neutral.

While eliminating systematic risk is straightforward conceptually, it is less simple in practice.[16] Controlling long/short portfolio risk using commercially available optimizers can be an unstable process, requiring a level of precision that may be beyond the current capability of many optimization algorithms and risk models. Also, the risk added by deviations from market neutrality can be difficult to measure *ex ante*.

The optimization process typically creates downward-biased estimates of the optimized portfolio's true risk characteristics. This is because optimizers maximize errors by overusing statistical estimates of small variances and small or negative correlations when minimizing risk. The end result is that "optimized" portfolios often have significantly more risk than estimated. Market risk may thus be a substantial part of the risk of many "market-neutral" long/short portfolios.

A related issue is whether market-neutrality is conceptually consistent with active management. Market neutral implies that the portfolio is not exposed to systematic risk factors. For active strategies based on systematic-risk-factor tilts, truly neutralizing the portfolio's systematic risk may imply that the portfolio has little, if any, active return.[17]

---

16. See R. Michaud, "The Markowitz Optimization Enigma," *Financial Analysts Journal,* January/February 1989 for discussion of these and other optimization issues.
17. I am indebted to F. J. Gould for this perception.

Forecast Reliability Risk

It is important to note that a long/short strategy does not increase the level of information in a forecast. It does, however, typically increase the level of active risk assumed by an investor. Consequently, a long/short strategy may add substantial "forecast reliability" or "information level" risk to the investment process.[18] A long/short strategy that uses an unreliable forecast can dramatically increase the probability of large losses.

The appropriate level of active risk assumed by an investor should be related to the reliability of the forecast. Given the forecast reliability of many stock forecasts, the level of residual risk typically associated with long-term institutional portfolios may often be optimal.

Trading Profits

Many long/short managers monitor and alter portfolio structure in real time. Such procedures can reduce margin and cash-reserve costs. Continuous portfolio monitoring also has the potential for capturing trading profits that may be otherwise unavailable. The net effect may be to raise the height of the fixed-cost efficient frontier in Figure 4–2. However, many long-only managers also monitor and trade portfolios in real time.

Utility Issues

Can long/short strategies be of particular benefit to some classes of investors?

Certain investment styles may be particularly advantaged by long/short strategies. In particular, small-stock portfolios are often index-constrained even at low levels of residual risk. A long/short strategy may enable a small-stock investor to efficiently increase active risk. However,

---

18. I am indebted to Robert Michaud for this observation.

potential benefits may be mitigated by the trading costs of shorting small stocks.

One feature of market-neutral long/short strategies is flexibility with respect to asset allocation decisions. A long/short strategy employing bond futures can be used for cash management, for example. Fund policy and active asset allocation decisions can be made independent of the decision to use a long/short manager. The strategy allows unbundling of market timing and stock selection decisions. A critical issue is whether such features are worth the costs and whether suitable alternatives are available. In particular, long-only managers can employ many futures overlay strategies to structure a wide variety of return patterns for various client preferences.

Small pension funds, wealthy individuals, and corporate cash managers, for example, may find the strategy attractive, in part because small fund size may limit the consequences of portfolio risk in the context of other sources of wealth.

A short investment horizon limits risk. Traders and opportunistic short-term investors may find a long/short strategy useful.

Finally, the strategy may be an ideal vehicle for maximizing the impact of unusually reliable (presumably short-term) information.

The issue is, ultimately, one of investor utility. The appropriateness of the risk and return of a long/short strategy can depend on the context of current asset values, liabilities, and investment policy. However, if the objective is simply to increase alpha by increasing active risk, many institutional investors have a number of viable alternatives. Active risk can be increased by eliminating investment in passive funds and low-risk asset classes and by increasing the size of funds allocated to normal active managers. The availability of such simple alternatives may affect the attractiveness of long/short strategies for long-term institutional investors.

CONCLUSION

A long/short strategy is not an economic free lunch. Increases in active return are generally accompanied by increases in active risk. Claims of superiority often reflect misunderstandings of basic principles of modern finance and/or the hybrid character of the strategy. The investment benefits of the long/short strategy derive primarily from leverage and possible increases in the active return-risk ratio stemming from less index-constrained portfolios. When additional costs are included, efficient long-only portfolios may dominate long/short portfolios at levels of risk normally associated with institutional active management.

If sell inefficiencies exist, both long and long/short managers are in a position to exploit them, raising the question of the persistence and economic significance of such inefficiencies. If long/short managers have exclusive access to exploitable inefficiencies, it may fall in the domain of trading profits based on real-time portfolio monitoring; however, many long-only portfolio managers also monitor and trade portfolios in real time.

Long/short strategies are part of the continuum of active investment strategies. They may be useful in increasing the reward-risk ratio of relatively high-active-risk portfolios. However, because long/short investing does not increase a forecast's information level, it may expose an investor to substantial "forecast reliability" risk. Given the current state of investment technology and implied levels of risk, the suitability of the strategy for long-term institutional investors is an open issue.

Long/short investing may be most appropriate for special situations and hedge funds—that is, for certain investment styles, small portfolios, traders, and other short-term investors or when highly reliable information is available. However, the likely increase in portfolio risk must be considered in the context of objectives, liabilities, costs, and alternatives.

Let:[19]

w_i = portfolio weights, $\Sigma w_i = 1$,
b_i = index weights, $\Sigma b_i = 1$,
z_i = $w_i - b_i$ = over- and under-weights, $\Sigma z_i = 0$,
z_i^+ = $\{z_i$ if > 0, 0 otherwise$\}$, $\Sigma z_i^+ = c$ and
z_i^- = $\{z_i$ if<0, 0 otherwise$\}$.

The quantity Σz_i^+ represents investment in the over-weighted or "long" part of an active portfolio; Σz_i^- represents investment in the underweighted or "short" part of an active portfolio. By definition, $\Sigma z_i^+ = -\Sigma z_i^- = c$. For an index fund, $c = 0$. From this point of view, a long portfolio is an unleveraged long/short portfolio, which is reflected in the fact that c is generally much less than one. Because a long/short strategy is typically less index-constrained, the value of c in the short portfolio of a long/short strategy can be much larger than for a long-only portfolio.[20] The value of c also depends, in part, on the level of residual risk assumed.

To estimate the residual risk of normal active institutional portfolios, let:

R^2 = portfolio R-squared,
σ_ε = portfolio residual risk, or standard deviation,
σ_M = market risk (standard deviation),
NA = the normal active long-only institutional portfolio,

If:

$R^2 = 0.95$,
$\sigma_M = 16\%$ and
$\beta_P = 1$,

---

19. See C. B. Garcia and F. J. Gould, "The Generality of Long-Short Equitized Strategies," *Financial Analysts Journal,* September/October 1992 for further details.
20. See footnote 6.

then:

$$\sigma_\varepsilon(NA) = 3.5\% \text{ and}$$
$$\sigma_P = 16.4\%$$

where

$$\sigma_\varepsilon = \left[\beta_p \times \sigma_M / R\right] \times \sqrt{\left(1 - R^2\right)} \text{ and}$$
$$\sigma_P = \beta_P \times \sigma_M / R.$$

Based on estimates in footnote 9, three is a reasonable multiplier of the residual risk of a normal active portfolio with respect to a long/short portfolio.[21]

21. I thank F. J. Gould, Robert Michaud, V. D'Silva, J. Scott, R. Ferguson, and D. Stein for their helpful comments.

Financial Analysts Journal

The *Financial Analysts Journal* is a bimonthly publication combining scholarly rigor with the point of view of an investment practitioner. It is the flagship publication of the Association for Investment Management and Research (AIMR), developers and administrators of the prestigious Chartered Financial Analyst (CFA®) designation for investment professionals.

The *Journal* regularly taps the best minds in the field for its editorial content. All articles must meet the high standards of the publication's distinguished editorial board while remaining useful to its sophisticated readers. The *Journal* thus includes a variety of investment-related topics in each issue and does not organize its contents around central themes.

In today's rapidly changing financial world, it is more important than ever to keep up with the pace of the investment industry. Each bimonthly issue features articles on leading-edge topics by renowned investment professionals. One of the most respected periodicals in its field, with over 30,000 readers worldwide, the *Journal* will be a valuable addition to your library.

Start your subscription today!

For more information, or to receive a catalog of AIMR publications, please contact:

AIMR
P. O. Box 3668
Charlottesville, VA 22903
Tel: (804) 980-3668
Fax: (804) 980-9755
E-mail: info@aimr.com
Web site: http://www.aimr.com/aimr.html

5

⑥ ALTERNATIVE QUANTITATIVE APPROACHES TO LONG/SHORT STRATEGIES

Russell J. Brooks
Principal
Market Profile Theorems, Inc.

We believe a long/short investment strategy is appropriate for consideration by institutional equity investors and conservative individuals to provide consistently attractive rates of return in both up and down market environments, and at acceptable risk-reward levels. We further believe the remainder of the 1990s will present great opportunities in adding value to returns using a series of such long/short strategies. Accordingly, while performance is the end we all seek, it should not stop us from asking *why* this particular approach works. It is by asking this question that we develop a deeper understanding of *how* markets work, leading to more discriminating models and better performance.

MARKET NEUTRAL

The Long and Short of It

The riskiest parts of the investment in stocks are the stock market itself and the tendency to apply too much subjectivity to the selection process. A large portion of the gains in stocks, whether long or short, is conditional on the movement of the market. Hence, the skill of the investment manager to produce gains above and beyond the standardized averages depends on three factors: one, taking advantage of the correct market style, thus being in the right sectors and industries; two, bringing value-added performance at the margins using several complimentary models; and three, proper asset allocation among stocks, bonds, and cash.

Our modeled, hard-wired approach takes away some of the basic tenets of poor judgment. In other words, it eliminates feelings from overcoming good reasoning, and prevents taking shortcuts that overstep sound logic. Since human beings can only digest five to seven different things at once, a robust methodology can eliminate illogical behavior. Accordingly, a solid long/short, market-neutral strategy eliminates the effective escape behavior, which is often accomplished through the simple adjustment of equity allocation.

Logical Concept

Good judgment comes from experience, and a lot of that comes from bad judgment.

It is possible to develop and employ quantitative equity models which possess the ability to produce superior rates of return. It is our position that the emergence of value, and its recognition, are dynamic processes. The models that we employ to produce superior returns seek to both identify and measure the market's response to value. The combination of style identification, insider activity, earnings expectations, and technical strength form the basis of a solid stock selection process. This philosophy drives our proprietary investment approach and continues to feed opportunities into the product pipeline.

Oscillations in the marketplace create operational inefficiencies that are the principles for exploiting excess price performance. These are not anomalies and thus need not be explained away. The multifactor model that will be examined on the following pages provides the linkage to these excess returns. A sound methodology brings continuity and durability to the investment process because it is less dependent on people than are the more traditional approaches. Although not bulletproof, the combination of models improves the propensity to pick stocks that will bring excess returns to the portfolio while controlling risk.

Other multiple core strategies can be overlaid to the basic long/short strategy. For example, one could easily reduce risk by stacking S&P futures onto the fund, or tilting index funds. As Albert Einstein once opined, "Imagination is more important than knowledge."

THE QUANTITATIVE CHALLENGE

Genius and Perspiration

The irrepressible comic and observer of the human condition, George Burns, reportedly received the following letter from a fan: "I seem to be having a hard time getting ahead in life. The other day I read that Thomas Edison once said, 'Genius is 1 percent inspiration and 99 percent perspiration.' Do you believe that?" Mr. Burns responded by saying: "I'm not sure Edison ever said that. All I know is the last time I danced with him he could have used a can of Right Guard."

Certainly over the past 10 years the investment research community has been presented with a good deal of new inspiration. Techniques such as nonlinear and conditional approaches have provided exciting alternatives to the modeling process. Specifically, the researcher is now armed with neural nets, decision trees, chaos theory, fuzzy logic, and genetic algorithms, to name a few. Better sampling techniques using holdout populations are also available.

This plethora of inspiration has not simplified the job of the quantitatively oriented modeler, with the amount of perspiration generated growing in at least exponential proportions. The increasing complication places an additional incumbency on the researcher to understand not only the technical implementation and applications of each of the new techniques, but also their strengths and weaknesses. For example, while neural nets have the advantage of uncovering previously unknown correlations, "overtraining" can result in what one researcher has termed "artificial stupidity" wherein relationships and data inferences become nonsensical.

It has been our experience in general, and specifically in the development of the model presented later in the chapter, that the best insights, discoveries, and results are the product of combining traditional analysis with some of the newer quantitative methods. For example, we took advantage of the traditional methods of isolating groups of companies into value/growth, and of defining different market environments in a similar manner. However, we availed ourselves of newer statistical techniques such as information coefficients to allow us to include outliers in our population. As a corollary to our experience, we therefore suggest that the successful *nouveau quant* must have the perspective and experience to combine the promising insights delivered by traditional analysis with the new quantitative platform.

The new quantitative world comes with the same pitfalls faced by traditional researchers, and is equipped with some new ones as well. To the problem of handling outliers, we add data mining and survivorship bias. A new problem, due in part to the enormous computing power available to today's *nouveau quant,* is that of combinational complexity ("overfitting" or "artificial stupidity").

It is no longer enough to determine what to buy or sell, but when. Assets that are clearly defined as containing value relative to other asset classes may lie unloved for long periods of time before their real values are recognized. Given the extraordinary gains in the U. S. equity markets over the past 12 years, the average investor has become increasingly jaded in expectations of 15-percent annual returns. Their patience in waiting for value to materialize has been shortened considerably. At the same time, a characteristic of equity markets in 1994 and 1995 has been the rapid turnover in theme-focus, virtually on a month-to-month basis. Such an environment forces the emergence of models that offer better performance timing at the industry and sector level.

Clearly, multifactor modeling will become increasingly important to managers of assets. While there will continue to be the street-smart Warren Buffets and Mario Gabellis of the world, their highly focused approach on just a few stocks or industries is by definitition limited to a narrow universe, and subject to the risk associated with the assumptions used to arrive at the selection of a futuristic theme as an investing Magna Carta. (That's another way of saying that the interactive couch potato has all his or her eggs in one basket.) The vast majority of money will continue to be allocated to a broader universe of investments. While the approaches of persons like Buffet and Gabelli have clearly added value, the economic realities of managing vast oceans of capital will force the broader use and development of quantitative modeling techniques. Further, the combination of submodels and factors in the asset selection and allocation process will become increasingly important.

Contrary to popular opinion, the combination of new technology and quantitative techniques has not made the job of the equity researcher easier. As the prior discussion indicates, both the requirement for grasping a broader knowledge base and additional problems come with this new frontier. On one level, it is our hope that these new tools can provide models which create value-added returns for investors. The early results of the specific model presented in the remainder of this chapter are heartening in this regard. On another, and more important level, it is our fervent hope that these tools allow us to ask new and better questions.

A Live Example

The basis for developing the four-factor model presented on the following pages included both traditional and quantitative techniques. Much of the inspiration was derived from contacting the academic and investment world and testing the hypotheses and results that they generated. For example, the work of Rundleman, Latne, and Jones was an important jumping-off point for the expectational earnings submodel. In allowing researchers to point us in promising directions, we saved much time in model development. What remained was to retest their results and bring them up-to-date, given new data acquired since publishing. Finally, we added enhancements to their basic thesis, thus adding performance. In some cases the enhancements made all the difference between real-world excess returns and questionable outcomes. This approach was applied to developing the market style, insider, earnings, and technical submodels. As a final step, the individual models were combined into a supermodel, which serves as the primary input for selecting issues for inclusion in both long and short portfolios.

In the modeling process, both traditional and new quantitative techniques were applied. Every effort was made to eliminate or reduce survivorship bias, to include outliers, and to avoid artificial stupidity. The survivorship bias problem has been significantly reduced as real-time model results have been collected within our own database and analyzed. In fact, one could divide our research process into two stages: one, the initial, when reliance on such statistical techniques such as holdout sampling were very important; and the second (when the real-time results derived from our models were generated over time and available to us) in which we could better control for survivorship bias, etc. The combination of the submodels required a sensitivity to not overtrain and to avoid data mining. Finally, it was important to select for independence in the performance of the submodels from one another.

The careful planning and execution of our model development has paid off. The performance of the real-time model, in place and verifiable from data sent to clients starting in the fall of 1989, has matched or exceeded that predicted theoretically. It is quite often the case that academic theory is difficult to apply in real-time markets. We generally found such slippage when we retested or brought forward the models developed in the academic world. Often this shortfall occurred as a result of underestimating total transaction costs (including market impact, commissions, and acquirability-in-size), not accounting for survivorship bias, data mining, poor or inadequate sampling techniques, and the avoidance of outliers.

Some differences exist between our theoretical expectations and the real-time results. For example, like the findings of so many other researchers, evidence exists that the algorithms behind our models are not linear. That is to say, while in general the lowest (worst) model scores provide the worst returns, and the best deciles the strongest results, the transition is not smooth, not linear. Intervening breakpoints provide more uneven returns. This suggests to us that a nonlinear mechanism may be at work here, and it will undoubtedly prove useful to seek an answer to this new question. We are in the process of applying some quantitatively nonlinear techniques to this observation at the present time.

Genesis of a Style-Correlated Strategy
Discussion of strategy models must begin with common understanding and definitions.

Market Profile Model   This multifactor model evaluates the market pricing mechanism for individual stock factors (characteristics), enabling identification of prevailing style preferences. Information coefficients (ICs) drawn from this methodology reveal the underlying patterns of premiums associated with detecting the broader trends, inconsistencies, and inefficiencies.

Insider Activity Model   The model employs analysis of buying and selling by corporate insiders to help reduce risk. The algorithm includes seven proprietary discriminators and weighting components, based on the intuitive and tested premise that insider activity holds information content not available in the marketplace.

Earnings Expectational Model   The earnings model measures the impact and probability of "earnings surprise" through the use of various consensus earnings estimates. Standardized unexpected earnings (SUE) theory is the basis of the algorithm, which is enhanced using a six-factor model. Residual value-added price performance, generated from positive and negative surprise modeling, is a proven technique.

Technical Model   This model is generated by analyzing relative strength of stock price and volume, as well as by applying a proprietary algorithm that produces an overbought/oversold indicator. It provides an input consistent with portfolio managers' longer-term investing horizons.

Summary Model   A proprietary compilation, the summary model combines the *market profile, insider, earnings,* and *technical* methodologies. By combining models which provide such diverse real-time views of market valuations, market risk is kept low relative to excess returns, causing the statistical measures of risk/reward to improve. The combination of the four models achieves a dynamic perspective on value. This result, expressed in the summary model, yields risk-adjusted excess returns greater than that of any of the single models.

MARKET PROFILE

Factor Analysis

It is not enough to just follow relative strength and trending patterns. Soon after we began building our research, we realized that not only did there appear to be different sensitivities among market factors (characteristics), but both a trending mechanism and mean regression were at work. In building our knowledge database, we developed average values for each of these factors. We currently use these to find the degree to which the current month's scores are over/under valued. In the current *market profile* model, a total of 10 factors are scored to create a ranking for each of 2,400 issues which takes into account the current market bias. Volatility is therefore moderated by a 10-factor approach, and interpretation is supplemented by insight into the degree of overall variation of the 10 factors from their historical means. We have also developed rules for evaluating the broad market bias for value and earnings-driven/momentum environments using cumulative, relative scores for each of the factors.

Relative Values

Another reason to include market style is the consistency it brings to the stock selection process. For example, one would not build a coast-to-coast railroad and leave off 100 miles of track in the middle. In studying value and growth derivative products being marketed worldwide, we are struck by the narrow scope of research. For instance, most of the derivative products currently available use as their genesis, the S&P/BARRA value-growth spread. Simply put, they merely divide a factor representing differences in returns of securities with different price/book ratios.

A number of objections can be made to this relatively simple interpretation. First and foremost, this design uses only one classification measurement—current price to book. This breakpoint is selected so that slightly more than half the issues selected are value, and the other growth. Between these division points, stocks are assigned to portfolios that remain the same, simply by placing them in one portfolio or another based on a stock's price to book ratio. Price to book only represents one-tenth of our *market profile* model. Thus, by taking the factors that we use in this model and studying historical graphs and data associated with them, one gains a better perspective and sense of continuity relating to the question of value versus growth.

INSIDER ACTIVITY

The basic assumption underlying insider activity is that individuals who are running corporations have a special understanding of their companies' fortunes. As a society, we have decided that in allowing these persons to buy and sell publicly held stock there exists the potential for abuse. However, more important, we believe that it is more a healthy expression of the entrepreneurial spirit that the people running the company own shares. As a matter of fact, investors should take it as a positive sign when company managers have their own money at stake. To prevent abuses inherent in this process, there are constraints on such trading. For example, an insider must declare open market transactions before the one tenth day of the month following the month in which the transaction was made, in effect creating a maximum as a 41-day window for declaration.

Interpretation

Insider activity data, and their interpretation, continues undergoing mutation. For instance, the quality of the data and related reporting systems continually improves. Additionally, as a firm, we clean up the data on a weekly basis, eliminating many casual errors and thus producing one of the most effective insider-activity databases in existence.

One problem inherent in analyzing insider activity is that the data rely on so many inputs before getting to the modeling process. The insider must report the transaction in a timely manner; he or she must know how to properly fill out the SEC reporting forms, and a government or private-sector employee must transpose the form to a computer. We estimate the current error rate to be as high as 20 percent. Recently, the filing task has been taken much more seriously, with the resultant transactions being reported in a more timely manner. This trend has accelerated and seems to coincide with some of the changes in reporting requirements instituted in early 1992.

Information Content

Some researchers perceive that, because the data may be in better condition, insider activity contains less information content, producing less stock-price-performance advantage to investors, than it did in years past. This has not been our experience.

A large contingent of money managers, technicians, and analysts closely monitor insider buyers and sellers for clues to a company's success and the future direction of its stock price. Some academic studies attempting to prove or disprove the insider advantage have concluded that insiders as a whole do only slightly better than would be expected on the basis of chance in predicting the direction of their company stock. However, one must keep in mind two facts concerning the results of our *insider* model. First, the most-significant price performance enters into the very top and very bottom deciles of our work. Second, the sophisticated algorithm that we employ asks many more questions than that of just the simple, casual transaction. We have proven that a strong multifactor model that removes the smoke and mirrors of many insider transactions can prove extremely productive at the margins. Furthermore, the combining of this methodology with our other models produces a powerful and more predictive investment tool.

Insider Investment Results

The examination of performance for the *insider* model as a stand-alone outcome looked at performance using calculations for mean absolute and excess returns, standard deviation of returns, and model persistence of returns for 1, 2, 3, 6, and 12 months, as well as model failure. The excess returns of fractiles within both 20 percent and 10 percent divisions are virtually identical, and provide positive delta. The same performance continuum is even stronger for finer divisions of the top 10-percent fractile when more subjective fine-tuning is added on a weekly updated basis.

Different market environments provide different excess return patterns vis-à-vis our *insider* model. The graph in Figure 5–1 presents results from a more refined selection formula whereby weekly changes in insider behavior produce what we view are the very best current opportunities.

The performance of the companies selected (buy and sell) were from a universe of 2,423 issues during a time period between April 1994 and June 16, 1995. While the spread between buys and sells yielded a positive delta in favor of buys, the nature of the spread differed over the market environment. There was a consistent, positive delta over the entire period. This result was most pronounced during the time of gradually rising prices, and less wide during the dynamic price advance experienced from December 1994. In both the overall period and the time of gradually rising prices, there existed a positive expected delta in both buy and sell portfolios relative to the market averages.

These results are very consistent with our long-term backtests on insider activity as we model it. In essence:

1. The *insider* model is actionable at the margin and for at least 19-week holding periods.

2. Companies with insider buying outperform both those with insider selling and the market.

3. Companies with insider selling tend to underperform both those with insider buying and the market.

4. Different market environments provide different results, with rapidly rising markets yielding more modest outcome vis-à-vis Market Profile Theorems's *insider* model.

5. Insider selling tends to underperform in all markets.

EARNINGS EXPECTATIONS

The group of individuals second-closest to the fortunes of publicly held companies are the analysts who work for brokerage firms, banks, money management companies, or

FIGURE 5-1

Performance and Duration of Actionable Insider Signals, 4/17/94–6/16/95

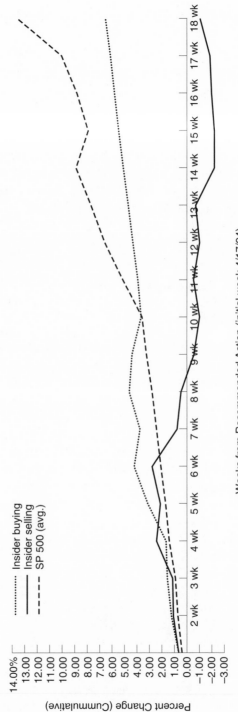

private research boutiques. These analysts provide research to clients (both institutional and retail), to their investment banking arms, and to each other. Studies on the
information content of earnings estimates, both immediate and long term, have found residual value in acting on
certain configurations of their estimates. The residual
value (excess over- or underperformance) has been generated by two classes of data provided by analysts: (1) the
degree to which the estimates are different from the most-
recently reported number; and (2) the direction of analyst
estimates.

Standardized Unexpected Earnings

Much of the pioneering work on estimates as a guide to future performance was done by three researchers, Latne,
Rundelman, and Jones. While others concentrated on simple earnings surprise (the percent difference in the mean
analyst earnings estimate and the actual earnings at the
time of the reported earnings), these individuals put forth
the more sophisticated concept of standardized unexpected
earnings (SUE), comparing the mean earnings estimate
over a period of time before the estimate to the actual earnings reported, and then standardizing it statistically (divid-
ing the result by the standard deviation of estimates).

In sum, the research suggested that, in general, the
degree of difference between the estimate and the actual
earnings number is directly proportional to the relative
price move in the stock. While this result is not unexpected,
what was surprising was that relative price performance
persisted in the same direction (but with lessening impact)
for many weeks and months after the disparity was re-
vealed. Accordingly, an investor could take long-term advantage of an earnings announcement.

There are many corollaries to this concept, all serving
to lessen the strength of the strict form of the efficient market hypothesis (EMH). For example, residual value has
been found in the direction of mean analyst estimates, and

in simple, quarterly earnings surprise. All are combined in our earnings expectational model.

Psychological Phenomenon

Besides the obvious parallel precedent in popular Wall Street lore that an investor should act immediately to sell a stock that disappoints the investor's expectation, we also have some insights as to why this phenomenon works. This primarily addresses the psychological occurrence of cognitive dissonance and the political nature of the analysts' decision-making process.

Cognitive dissonance refers to the refusal of an individual or group with an established opinion to accept another point of view, in spite of new irrefutable evidence suggesting quite another conclusion. The stronger their original opinion, the more resistant they are to changing it. Further, whether in science, politics, or the investment world, the more highly regarded the person or institution providing the opinion, the greater the cognitive dissonance of the majority accepting the opinion. In the investment community, not only are analysts unwilling or slow to change, but investors who rely on high-profile analysts are as well. We believe this factor creates prolonged inefficiency in the pricing mechanism of individual stocks.

The *political nature* of the analysts' environment works to create inefficiencies generated by earnings surprise. (We won't include a discussion of the impact of what we believe is a mythical wall between investment banking and stock recommendations at brokerage firms.) Very few investors have the psychological makeup to admit they are totally wrong. This applies to analysts as well, except that to do so might add the ignomiy of putting their credibility and, therefore, jobs on the line. What tends to occur is that analysts will gradually cut back or increase estimates as appropriate over a period of time following strong disparity between estimates and actual earnings. This tends to prolong disappointment/optimism, which creates longer-term pressure on prices in the corresponding direction. The result is that pricing tends to be less discreet and more drawn out in nature. Evaluation of trends in the direction of estimates provides evidence that this type of activity is occurring and can also be used to anticipate reversals in trends (when the trend slows or reverses).

Because the research we have done over the past eight years confirms certain aspects of earnings expectational theory, we include an *earnings expectation* model in the long/short strategy.

TECHNICAL MODEL

The explosion in the variety of technical analytic techniques employed over the past 10 years has been truly astounding. This has been driven in large part by the development and distribution of computer and communications technology which have allowed for virtually instantaneous transmission of worldwide transactions to trading rooms, offices, and homes. Furthermore, once transmissions are received, individuals now have the power to process the information in an infinite array of algorithmic combinations, and have access to increasingly sophisticated communications channels through which to act (trade) on their conclusions. It is commonly expressed among senior money managers that pricing processes, which 20 years ago took weeks to wash through the marketplace, now take hours.

Categories

Most technical models fall into two categories: pattern recognition, and analysis of price and volume. We suppose one could argue that they are one in the same, and indeed, with the application of computers to pattern recognition, the boundary has become blurred. Three models come to mind in the area of pattern recognition—Edwards &

Magee's, Elliot & Prechter's, and Market Profile (Chicago), which is used on the CBOT by many traders. Examples of price and volume approaches would include: price trending models, overbought/oversold models, stochastics, parabolics, regression models, moving averages, envelopes, DMI, ADX, Bollinger bands, MACD, RSI, on-balance volume, divergences, and chaos theory.

Relative Trends

We have constructed our *technical* model simply and with a longer-term "portfolio manager's time horizon," and have chosen the approach that relative trends in prices provide the most consistent, risk-adjusted, technical performance. While not spectacular, trend-following approaches used in the right markets (nonconsolidating types) offer a good deal of consistency. Given the general long-term tendency of the equity markets to trend higher, the odds would favor this type of approach in the long run. We have combined this concept with a *technical* model for individual stock selection that evaluates relative price strength over 4-week, 12-week, and 24-week time periods. In addition, we evaluate volume over the two most recent 4-week periods. The ideal stock from our perspective has positive relative strength for all three periods on increasing average volume.

While this model has not been the most spectacular of the approaches, it has lent stability to the *summary* model and improved the performance of both it and other models combined with it.

SUMMARY MODEL

Style shapes the pattern of excess investment returns more consistently than practically any other components of decision-making conduct. Variability in the market is even more important than a simple exploration of price-to-book valuation by itself. When balanced, inclusive style analysis is combined with the independent variables of the *insider*, *earnings*, and *technical* models, and a powerful and stable methodology emerges. The important goal of reducing the impact of style alone on performance is achieved. In other words, a model-driven/market-linked (MDML) approach emerges. It is from this arena that both our long and short portfolios take there cue.

Long/Short Strategy

We believe that the common methods employed in most market-neutral strategies, and used to build portfolios for relative price performance, is a flawed process as there is often an override which seeks to equally weight or balance the industries and sectors.

The long/short model we have chosen is based on the concept that by analyzing correlations between all our models, a more natural filter produces stocks which are candidates for inclusion in long/short, market-neutral portfolios. Weightings are assigned based on the best and worst stocks.

One result of this unforced method is that of reducing risk. Another is that of improving the elusive butterfly of market and sector timing. In other words, our procedure eliminates the need to artificially weight sectors and industries, curtailing the danger of being either long or short the wrong issues or industries.

It is important to realize that this methodology is not foolproof, and that at times aggregate analysis can be more of an art. That is not to say we subjectively impact the "black box" algorithms that supply us with the best long and short conditions, but, when we analyze the results of the number crunching, it occasionally becomes necessary to impart our interpretation. These checks and balances can therefore be used to override portfolio positions in order to protect the clients' assets.

Dynamic Perspective on Value

We have found that the concepts that make our long/short program less synthetic than more common market-neutral approaches, and the reasons for the exceptional dynamic perspective on value as well as steady performance, are related to the assumptions which drive the *summary* model.

1. There is an informational hierarchy in the marketplace for stocks that cannot possibly, in a practical sense, be known, understood, and acted upon at the same time by the investment public. [*Insider* and *Earnings Expectational* models]

2. Human beings, and the psychology that drives them, are a major factor in setting prices. For example, investors tend to ignore initial and surprising bad news, and in fact are paralyzed by it. [*Earnings Expectational* model]

3. It is important to understand the factors that are driving stocks as they relate to those components by which we measure fundamentals such as PEs, earnings growth, and dividend yield. [*Market Profile* and *Technical* models]

4. Markets trend in the long run. [*Technical* and *Market Profile* models]

5. Markets revert to the mean. [*Market Profile* and *Insider* models]

6. Relative strength is important. [All models]

Performance: The Ultimate Goal

Managers of investments are ultimately judged by their ability to win above-average returns for their clients. This is no different in the management of equities in particular. According to a survey done for *Pensions & Investments* by Richard Carton (August 3, 1992), plan sponsors score performance highest at 8.6 on a 10-point scale. Quality of personnel and firm reputation score 7.8 and 7.5 respectively, while fees were valued at 6.6 out of 10 in importance in the selection of a manager. Turnover was not evaluated.

It is against this unrelenting expectation of superior performance that the investment management community has labored over the past five years. The Rock of Sisyphus has become larger, and the hill steeper, during this period. Rotation of group/sector performance has been unruly, margins slimmer across the entire investment community, and investors increasingly jaded by the extraordinary gains, averaging over 30 percent per year, from 1982 to 1990 (Dow Jones Industrial Average 750 to 3000). Over the seven-year period, our *summary* model has been available to the investment community; it has provided calm, relative performance gains in the eye of the swirling investment hurricane.

While our approach has proved valuable over the past seven years of actual implementation and 22 years of theoretical testing, we realize we may have only captured a healthy wedge of performance time. Accordingly, we have selected models that contain information content that transcends performance time frames—in other words, those that do well in most market environments, and which autocorrect to reflect underlying change in preference.

6

⑥ USING A
NONPARAMETRIC
APPROACH
TO MARKET-NEUTRAL
INVESTING

Geoffrey Gerber, Ph. D.
President
Twin Capital Management, Inc.

Market-neutral investing covers a wide spectrum of product offerings. This chapter focuses on one specific area: long/short equity portfolios based on a quantitative approach. The typically used linear multifactor valuation approach will be compared to a nonparametric or nonlinear methodology.

TYPICAL QUANTITATIVE APPROACH

One of the most common approaches used by active quantitative equity managers is the linear multiple factor valuation model. In this approach, a manager's value added comes from

1. Selecting the right factors;
2. Combining (possibly through forecasting) them into a composite alpha or ranking; and

The author would like to thank Jeff Jaffe, Wilfredo Palma and Tim Stack for their helpful and insightful comments and suggestions.

3. Constructing portfolios to maximize alpha while minimizing risk.

There are a number of advantages to linear factor valuation models. First, they have been well tested and documented in the financial literature.[1] Second, using multiple factors, the manager can focus on capturing anomalous returns on a "pure" basis (e.g., the effect of earnings/price ratios on returns net of the size effect). Third, linear factor models are often used for risk estimation. Therefore, many portfolio construction and performance attribution packages provide consistency across risk and return forecasting and performance attribution.

The typical linear multifactor model formulation is given by:

$$R_{i,t} = a_0 + b_{1,t} F_{1,i,t} + b_{2,t} F_{2,i,t} + \ldots + b_{k,t} F_{k,i,t} + e_{i,t} \quad (1)$$

where:

$R_{i,t}$ = Residual or total return for stock i during period t

$F_{k,i,z}$ = Factor k exposure for stock i at the beginning of period t

a_0 = Single (or distributed) constant

$b_{k,t}$ = Factor return for factor k during period t

$e_{i,t}$ = Unexplained return for stock i during period t

For each period, every stock's alpha (predicted return) is calculated by summing the products of the actual exposure $(F_{k,i,t})$ times the expected factor coefficient $(b_{k,t+1})$.

---

1. See, for example, Eugene F. Fama, and Kenneth R. French, "The Cross-Section of Expected Stock Returns," *Journal of Finance* 47 (June 1992), pp. 427–65; Eugene F. Fama and Kenneth R. French, "Common Risk Factors in the Returns on Stocks and Bonds," *Journal of Financial Economics* 33 (February 1993), pp. 3–56; S.P. Kothari, Jay Shanken, and Richard Sloan, "Another Look at the Cross-Section of Expected Stock Returns," *Journal of Finance* 49 (March 1995), pp. 185–224; Josef Lakonishok, Andrei Shleifer, and Robert W. Vishny, "Contrarian Investment, Extrapolation, and Risk," *Journal of Finance* 49 (December 1994), pp. 1541–78.

Potential Pitfalls

There are potential pitfalls when using models related to equation (1). Various statistical tests can minimize some of these concerns, while alternative methodologies may be needed to address other concerns.

The first potential pitfall lies in the measurement error of the factor exposures $(F_{k,i,t})$. Financial databases, while perhaps expansive, are not necessarily free of inaccuracies. While standardization techniques eliminate many errors, they also distort the distribution by pushing in true outliers toward the middle.

A second pitfall involves the number of independent variables. Money managers frequently say "the more factors the better," an approach that econometricians call the exploratory method (or more derisively the "everything but the kitchen sink" method). Econometricians argue that a few factors are likely to be significant in any sample if a large number of factors are used. Thus, a model will appear to have more predictive power than it actually has. The general rule for any regression in the social sciences is to "select only one indicator for each conceptual variable."[2] For example, in a long/short model, one might rank stocks on a value/growth continuum. Since value can be differentiated from growth via many factors (e.g., price-to-price earnings, market-to-book, past growth in sales), money managers might like to use all of the factors in the same regression. However, the above suggests that one factor should be used.

Even if multicollinearity is not a problem, the results of the regression are described in part by the factor coefficients $(b_{k,t})$, which themselves are point estimates. The "true" regression coefficient lies in a confidence interval around the point estimate. However, most managers will typically analyze the average or cumulative effect of the beta coefficients over time, focusing solely on the point es-

---

2. J. Scott Armstrong, *Long-Range Forecasting: From Crystal Ball to Computer,* 2nd edition, (Wiley Interscience: New York, 1985), p.196.

timate rather than the range. Unfortunately, while the point estimate may be positive, the range may well include negative values implying that the "true" relationship may actually be negative. Of course, the t-statistic of the beta coefficient is useful in determining whether the beta coefficient is the right sign and significant.

Alpha Calculation

To calculate a stock's expected return, or alpha, within the linear factor model framework, the manager needs to forecast the future (one period ahead) coefficient $(b_{k,t+1})$.[3] A stock's alpha $(A_{i,t+1})$ is the sum of the products of the expected beta coefficient times the current standardized factor exposure. This can be written algebraically as:

$$A_{i,t+1} = b_{1,t+1} F_{1,i,t+1} + b_{2,t+1} F_{2,i,t+1} + \ldots + b_{k,t+1} F_{k,i,t+1}$$

An advantage of this approach is the ability to produce a relative ranking based on multiple criteria. Even if a stock is negatively exposed to some desired characteristics, it may be highly positively exposed to other desired characteristics. Offsetting this advantage, however, is that each stock's alpha is computed by multiplying a factor exposure that may be subject to measurement error times a forecasted point estimate. Calculating a stock's alpha with factor coefficient forecasts adds more noise to an already noisy process.

IDENTIFICATION AND CAPTURE

The two critical elements in the active equity valuation process are identification and capture.

Identification of market inefficiencies and anomalies is the first step in the valuation process. An important question is whether the anomaly can be adequately described by a linear model. For example, if a manager were to sort his

---

3. A simple forecast of $b_{k,t+1}$ would be to take the average coefficient from some initial period through period t.

universe into deciles ranked on price/earnings (P/E) ratios, he may find that the tenth-lowest P/E decile outperforms the ninth-lowest, which itself outperforms the eigth, and so on. Alternatively, he may find that there is a lot of differential performance at the tails, but not a lot of discrimination in the middle deciles. Unfortunately, a linear model assumes that the positive relationship between low P/E and stock return is monotonic across the universe.

The second step attempts to capture the return differential with the least volatility. Many quantitative active equity managers use either heuristic rules or some form of an optimization algorithm for this task. However, in a recent article, Richard Grinold stressed a difficulty with optimizers.[4] Unless the alphas are appropriately adjusted for both volatility and the modeler's confidence, alphas will tend "to be eaten up." In other words, the realized alphas will be smaller than the estimated alphas.

LONG-ONLY VERSUS LONG/SHORT EQUITY

In the context of any long-only active equity process where the benchmark portfolio is well defined and generally static (e.g., the S&P 500), a linear factor valuation approach is a very useful framework. In these cases, building a portfolio that will closely replicate the major characteristics of the benchmark can take advantage of discriminatory information while maintaining tight active risk control. If, however, the goal is to add value through a long/short (market-neutral) approach, then the focus should be return differentiation rather than discrimination.

A long/short equity approach will be successful if there is reliable return differentiation at the tails of the universe. The relationship between exposure and return in the middle of the exposure distribution does not mean as

---

4. See Richard Grinold, "The Fundamental Law of Active Management," *Journal of Portfolio Management* (Spring 1989), pp. 30–37.

much to the long/short portfolio return as it does to the long-only portfolio return. For example, if we were to rank a universe of stocks into quintiles by their P/E ratios, then we care only about the return differential for the two extreme quintiles in a long/short portfolio. But if we were running a long-only portfolio, we may need to hold stocks in the second and third quintiles in order to match the benchmark characteristics (e.g., the beta of the portfolio). Therefore, in a long-only portfolio, one wants a stepladder relationship between P/E quintiles and return. Because of this difference, a nonparametric approach, as described below, is more appropriate for a long/short than a long-only porfolio.

A NONPARAMETRIC APPROACH

To better focus on the return differential of the tails, we first isolate the most important factors that drive stock return. We select from among 16 factors (cutting across the value, forecast growth/momentum, and technical dimensions) those which are mutually independent of the others.[5]

Using monthly observations from January 1980 through December 1992, we focus on the correlation matrix of factor exposures. We find three factors which are conditionally independent from all others. The other variables included in the matrix are all conditionally dependent on one or more of the three factors selected.

The three factors represent one from each category: a valuation factor, a forecast revisions or analyst sentiment factor, and a technical factor. For each factor, we sort our universe (of approximately 900 stocks each month) into two, three, four, and five groups.

---

5. The 16 factors are taken from an existing linear long/short factor model.

We perform both independent and dependent sorts for each factor. Independent sorts result in an unequal number of stocks in each portfolio, while dependent sorts result in portfolios of an equal number of stocks.

Our results are robust with respect to the sorting technique, but are affected by the number of groups. We find that most differentiation between tails occurs when each factor is sorted into three groups (terciles).

This dependent sorting process is described in Figure 6–1. Three factors are selected for their mutual independence. We first sort our 900-stock universe each month into the highest, medium, and lowest "buckets" (of approximately 300 stocks) ranked on the most independent factor. Each of these three portfolio buckets is then broken three ways by sorting based on exposure to the second-most-independent

F I G U R E   6–1

Dependent Sorting

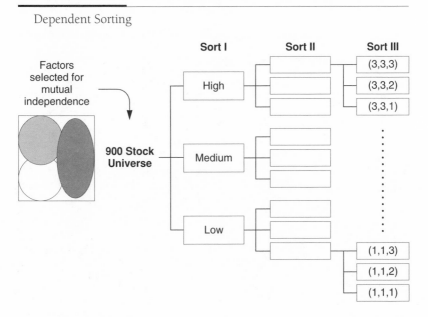

Source: Twin Capital Management, Inc.

FIGURE 6–2

Nonparametric Portfolio Simulation

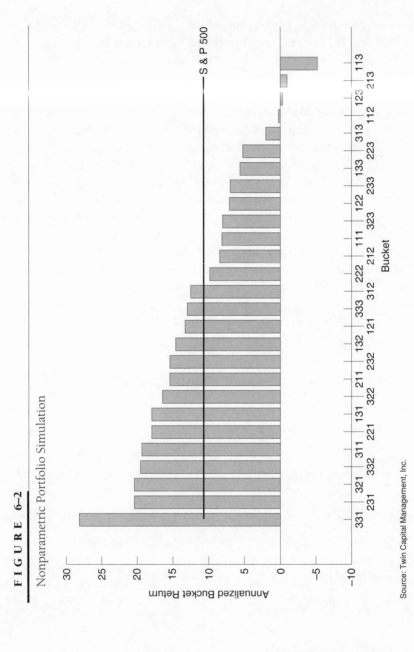

Source: Twin Capital Management, Inc.

factor. Finally, each of the nine portfolios is then again sorted using the third factor, resulting in 27 portfolio buckets with an equal number of stocks in each.

Each month, we measure the total return of the approximately 30 stock portfolios (equally weighted) for each of the 27 buckets. Figure 6–2 shows the annualized total return for each of the 27 bucket portfolios. The S&P 500 return is also shown as the horizontal line. Of the 27 buckets, 14 portfolios outperform the S&P 500 on a per year basis and 13 underperform.

The reader will notice that the best long stock bucket (331) is symmetrical with the best short bucket (113). The stocks most likely to outperform the market are highly exposed to the highest third of factors one and two and to the lowest third of factor one. Symmetry is not perfect at the tails, however, since four of the top five long-buckets have the highest third exposure to factor one, while only three of the top five short-portfolios have the lowest exposure to factor one.

Figure 6–2 covers the period from January 1981 through May 1995. When this long/short strategy was being researched and developed in 1993, we had calculated the portfolio returns through December 1992. One example of the strategy's robustness comes through the almost two-and-one-half-year update finding that 11 of the 12 tail buckets (that is, six long and six short) remained the best and worst, respectively. The one switch was the sixth-highest long bucket through December 1992, which became the seventh-highest-return long bucket through May 1995.

PORTFOLIO SIMULATIONS

Given the monthly returns and turnover for each of the 27 buckets, we simulated a number of long/short strategies. We analyzed the return (net of estimated transactions costs) and standard deviation for each simulation. The objective was to find the highest information ratio portfolio among the most realistic (based on risk and turnover criteria) simulations.

Since there are approximately 30 stocks in each of the 27 buckets, a strategy of buying the stocks in the best bucket and shorting the stocks in the worst bucket results in a portfolio of about 60 stocks. While this portfolio has excellent performance, the risk is relatively high. In addition, turnover exceeds 90 percent per month.

With three buckets on each side, we find much more reasonable risk levels, with still high (but diminishing) turnover. To further reduce turnover (at the cost of diminishing the return differential), we employ a "grandfather clause" rebalancing strategy. For example, if last month we shorted a stock in the 113 bucket and this month it moves into the 112 portfolio, then we would retain our short position. Even though its expected return is not as negative (relative to the market) as the expected return for another 113 replacement stock, the differential is not great enough to incur transaction costs.

The grandfather clause reduces the turnover to approximately 40 percent per month (per portfolio). While still high, this average monthly percentage has been most manageable through our real-time portfolio management experience.

Applying a 1 percent round-trip transaction cost for each of the long and short trades, returns for our final strategy are:

Period: January 1981—May 1995
Annualized (Long/Short)

Strategy value added:	15.19%
Active risk:	6.30
Average annual turnover:	465

While the average annual turnover is still quite high, value added far exceeds the 1 percent assumed round-trip cost.

COMPARISON OF NONPARAMETRIC TO LINEAR APPROACH

A comparison of the nonparametric long/short equity simulation to the simulated and real-time experience for the linear factor model approach bears at least two interesting findings. First, both the value added and the risk is lower for the linear approach (which uses an optimizer to build portfolios and minimize risk) than for the nonparametric approach. Given that the annual value added is so much higher, the nonparametric long/short equity strategy has a higher Sharpe and information ratio than does the linear factor approach.

Perhaps the most interesting observation is the total lack of correlation between the value added of the two strategies. The correlation between the monthly value added for the two approaches is only 0.03. Even though both approaches include the same three factors, the final application yields different results. We cannot completely attribute this to just the difference in the number of factors (the linear approach may include up to 8 or 10 factors at any given time), or to differences in a linear versus nonparametric approach. There are other elements (e.g., portfolio construction) that may also have a significant impact on value added.

CONCLUSION

A nonparametric long/short strategy was developed by focusing on the most independent factors included in an already existing linear multiple factor model. A comparison of the two approaches finds that the nonparametric approach may provide a higher information ratio. More important, the two approaches produce uncorrelated value added, implying that the two methodologies are distinct enough to be considered alternatives.

CHAPTER

7

⑥ # DIVERSIFYING MARKET-NEUTRAL STRATEGIES

Jane Buchan
Director and Portfolio Manager
Collins Associates

What is market-neutral investing? In some institutional circles, the term market neutral refers to a quantitative equity strategy where a long portfolio of undervalued stocks is held simultaneously with a short portfolio of overvalued stocks.[1] Ask certain sell-side investors about market-neutral investing and they may discuss convertible bond hedging. Yet other investors may assume you are talking about fixed-income basis trading. While many definitions abound, most center on the basic principle of *investing in one or more mispriced securities and hedging out the market risk.* Once the basic principle is uncovered and applied, it is apparent that there are many strategies which fit the definition.

BASIC CONCEPTS

Before discussing the details of the strategies which are contained in this broader definition, it is worth reviewing the basic concept. First, a group of securities are valued

---

1. For example, this is the perspective taken in Chapter 6.

relative to each other or some benchmark.[2] For example, Ford may be compared to Chrysler or the market as a whole, a Toyota warrant may be analyzed with respect to its underlying stock price and volatility, or a German post-office agency bond (Bundespost) may be compared to similar sovereign issues (Bunds). Adjustments may be made to reflect transaction costs including both direct expenses and market impact.

Once mispriced securities are identified, one of three types of positions is constructed. One approach is to purchase the undervalued securities and hedge the market risk by going short a fairly priced security. Usually, the short is an index future or the actual underlying stock in the case of a warrant or a convertible. If index futures are used, care must be taken that the portfolio of undervalued securities will track the index. Often this involves including only slightly cheap or even fairly priced securities in the long portfolio in order to ensure a sufficiently small tracking-error of the long undervalued portfolio with the hedging index.

A second approach is merely the reverse of the first approach. Overvalued securities are sold short, and the market risk is hedged by purchasing a fairly priced security (again, typically either an index future or the actual underlying stock). When shorting overvalued securities, care should be taken that the short position can be maintained for as long as the mispricing exists. If the mispricing increases, say because there continues to be abnormal demand for that particular class of stock, and the manager cannot maintain the short (e.g., a short-stock recall), then a loss will result even though the security may have been overvalued.

Finally, the third approach involves purchasing under-valued securities and shorting overvalued securities simultaneously. While on the surface this may seem like a trivial extension to the above approaches, there are some addi-

---

2. This is in contrast to absolute valuation measures such as the overall cheapness of a company.

tional issues with this "double alpha"[3] approach. First, in some markets, whole classes of securities may be under- or overvalued at any one time. Therefore, being both long and short may not be the optimal strategy. Second, particular attention needs to be paid to the tracking between the portfolios. While one may be comfortable either (a) buying undervalued small-cap stocks and hedging through the short sale of the Russell 2000 futures contract, or (b) shorting overvalued large cap stocks and hedging through the purchase of an S&P 500 future, a portfolio comprised of long small-cap stocks and short large-cap stocks can introduce a very substantial tracking error which may not be desired.[4] This could lead to negative returns for a while even though the individual securities might be properly classified as under- or overvalued.

This approach introduces a critical issue: At what point does a long-security versus short-security strategy degenerate into two directional positions and lose its market-neutral quality? The answer is arbitrary. Traditionally, strategies such as merger or risk arbitrage and long/short equity portfolio strategies have been considered to be market-neutral, although one could easily make arguments against such a position.

The return to merger or risk arbitrage, which involves purchasing the stock of a company being taken over while simultaneously shorting the stock of the acquiring company, is highly dependent on whether the merger deal is consummated. Unfortunately, if the deal is not completed, often the merger arbitrage position will result in a significant loss as the merger premium in the target company

---

3. Alpha is commonly referred to as the return due to nonmarket risk. Thus, it is often thought of as measuring the level of mispricing. A security with positive alpha is deemed to be undervalued and a security with negative alpha is deemed to be overvalued.
4. While this example may seem self-evident, the author has seen strategies with even greater tracking error between the two sides being represented as market neutral.

stock disappears. This return pattern of making a "good" return with consistency (as a high percent of mergers are completed), with the potential for a substantial downside in any one position, is not what many people think of when the term market neutral is generically used.

Likewise, some variants of the long/short equity portfolio strategy, which involves purchasing a basket of undervalued stocks while simultaneously shorting a portfolio of overvalued stocks, does not fit the generic definition of market neutral. A fundamental concept of market-neutral investing is that there is a "mispriced" security relative to another security or index. While many investors might agree that the bond basis is cheap or that the XYZ company convertible is overpriced versus its respective underlying stock, the designation of certain companies' stocks as cheap relative to other companies' stocks can lead to a level of subjectivity that, again, may not be what many people think of when the label market neutral is used.

On the other hand, strategies such as being long $1 million of Japanese yen and short $1 million of British sterling, or being long the German stock index (DAX) and short the French stock index (CAC) in equal dollar amounts, are not considered to be market neutral by most investors we have met, *even though they can be dollar-neutral on an investment basis.* This is because, in our opinion, *in order to be market neutral, a strategy must be neutral with respect to the main underlying exposure.*

As a starting point or guide, we consider the following strategies as market-neutral.

Market-Neutral Strategies

• Merger arbitrage	Long stock of company being acquired Short stock of acquiring company
• Long/ Short equity portfolios	Long a basket of undervalued stocks Short a basket of overvalued stocks in the same market
• Convertible bond hedging	Long cheap convertible bond Short underlying stock with the same net exposure

- Bond-basis hedging   Long (short) bond future
                              Short (long) underlying bond
- Different share classes   Long (short) ordinary share
                              Short (long) nonvoting share
- Mortgage hedging   Long mortgages
                              Short equivalent duration exposure
- Tight yield-curve trading   Long (short) 5-year government bond
                              Short (long) 7-year government bond
                              Long (short) 9-year government bond
                                with net zero duration

Strategies That Are Not Market Neutral

- Long/ short currencies   Long one currency
                              Short another currency in equivalent
                                dollar amount
- Spreads outside of directly Long one market (equity or fixed
  related markets   income)
                              Short another market (equity or fixed
                                income)
- General yield-curve trading Long (short) 20-year bond
                              Short (long) Treasury bill

Regardless of where one individually chooses to draw the boundaries on his or her own definition of market neutral, one should always keep in mind the well-worn phrase *caveat emptor*. Simply relying on someone's representation of a strategy as market neutral is not enough; instead one needs to ask, Why do you call this strategy market neutral?

THE MARKET-NEUTRAL UNIVERSE

What does the market-neutral universe look like? Using the above definition and data from the Collins Associates's manager universes, we have the real records for the following categories of managers.[5]

5. Collins Associates makes an attempt to include all qualified managers in its manager universes. The criteria for qualification are (a) real-time performance history (i.e., no back-tested or sample account data); and (b) willingness to report data on a real-time basis. This last qualification attempts to eliminate the bias of only including managers with good records. Thus, when a new manager is added to the database, the historical performance, even if it is real, is not included.

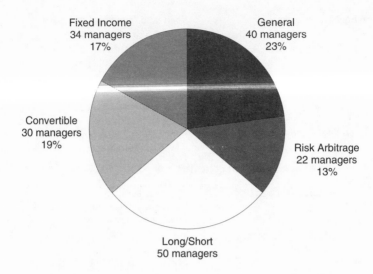

Risk or merger arbitrage, as discussed earlier, involves taking positions in merger transactions, spin-offs, and other corporate governance transactions. In order to fit into this category, managers must be participating in announced deals. For example, an investment manager who purchases a cheap stock in hope of a takeover would be excluded from this universe. What is considered an announcement of a transaction can include a very broad spectrum. In a few cases, an announcement will involve the specific terms of the transaction along with a time line, while at the other extreme, it may be as vague as "XYZ company has hired an investment banker to look for a buyer." Most of the managers included in the universe have mostly domestic portfolios. As of July 1, 1995, there were 22 risk arbitrage managers in the universe.

Long/short equity portfolio strategies were also discussed earlier. The substyles within this area run the gamut from short-term (i.e., daily) quantitative systems to longer-term (i.e., semiannual) fundamental systems. Unlike most of the other market-neutral investment managers, many of the practitioners come from the institutional side of the business and run much of their money on a separate account basis. Many of the investment managers in this universe also use their valuation methodology in a long-only version as well. In addition, a majority of the managers in this universe invest in domestic portfolios. As of July 1, 1995, there were 50 managers in this universe.

Convertible bond hedging involves, in its purest form, the simultaneous purchase of an undervalued convertible or warrant with the short sale of the underlying stock in a ratio which, for small-stock price moves, will result in zero net exposure to the company. Variants include purchasing a basket of warrants and convertibles and hedging with an appropriate stock-index contract, and inverting the strategy by selling short an overvalued convertible and purchasing the stock. Many of the investment managers tend to specialize in one of three areas: U.S. convertibles, Japanese warrants, or high-quality foreign convertibles. Most of the practitioners in this area tend to come from Wall Street where they were either convertible market-makers for their firms, traded proprietary capital, or some combination of both.[6] As of July 1, 1995, there were 30 managers in this universe.

Fixed-income arbitrage involves the trading of spread, basis, or yield curve risk. Examples include TED-spread trading, Eurodollar curve trading, butterflies in foreign sovereigns, cash versus swap spreads, off-the-run versus on-the-run Treasury bonds, and mortgage hedging. All of these trades involve the same underlying principle, which is net zero-duration exposure even if there is a nonparallel shift in the term structure. With the exception of the mortgage hedgers, managers tend to engage in a variety of transactions in many different markets. Barriers to entry are the highest in this area, as a minimum asset-size of as much as $20 million is often needed in order to gain access to the necessary credit lines. (In contrast, there have been many warrant traders who started business with $1 million or less under management.) Like the convertible hedgers, many of the practitioners come from Wall Street rather than the

---

6. Often, one of the consequences of this background is unfamiliarity with the institutional investment practices regarding portfolio disclosure, performance measurement, and marketing.

traditional institutional investment background. As of July 1, 1995, there were 34 managers in this universe.

Finally, there is a catch-all category, which we label general arbitrage. These are firms which typically engage in a variety of trades, although this universe does contain managers who have narrow styles but do not have a sufficient number of competitors to warrant a substyle classification of their own. Examples are an investment manager whose sole business is to "arbitrage" equity and fixed-income closed-end funds around the world, and another who trades the implied volatility in U.S. stock index options. The multifaceted managers in this universe tend to be larger in size and often contain several senior decision-makers. Some began in one style and, as they became more successful, added additional styles; others started with a diversified fund. Most of these managers can be thought of as some combination of the prior four categories. As of July 1, 1995, there were 40 managers in this universe.

PERFORMANCE CHARACTERISTICS OF THE UNIVERSES

For each of the substyles, we are able to compute performance characteristics. While these can be helpful in evaluating the strategies and managers, there are important qualitative factors which should also be considered.

Table 7–1 shows the quarterly returns, net of all investment manager fees, for the Collins's risk arbitrage composite universe. Table 7–2 gives the cross-sectional standard deviation for the quarter. For example, the average risk arbitrage investment manager in the universe returned 2.58 percent during the third quarter of 1992. Approximately two-thirds of the managers had returns between 0.42 percent and 4.74 percent for that quarter (i.e., the mean ± one standard deviation).

There are several interesting points which can be seen from the numbers. First, risk arbitrage, over the three years, performed the best as these universes are defined. What is also interesting to note is that, for the "average" manager, the better performance was not in 1994, even though this was

TABLE 7–1

Quarterly Composite of Managers by Substrategy

	Risk Arbitrage	Long/Short Equity	Convertible Hedging	Fixed-Income Hedging	General Hedging
3Q92	2.58%	1.58%	3.51%	0.32%	1.01%
4Q92	0.84	2.57	1.66	6.25	1.77
1Q93	6.60	4.73	3.45	4.06	4.89
2Q93	4.82	3.27	4.55	6.50	2.62
3Q93	4.31	3.61	3.76	5.54	4.95
4Q93	4.30	−0.28	2.60	5.19	5.14
1Q94	1.98	0.59	0.33	−6.75	2.26
2Q94	1.72	0.22	−2.30	0.95	2.22
3Q94	4.11	−0.05	1.55	2.64	−0.88
4Q94	0.40	2.18	−1.15	1.60	0.00
1Q95	4.17	1.53	2.84	3.51	3.74
2Q95	2.89	2.47	4.63	1.50	3.59
Average	**3.27%**	**1.82%**	**2.21%**	**2.60%**	**2.61%**

TABLE 7–2

Cross-Sectional Standard Deviation of Managers by Substrategy

	Risk Arbitrage	Long/Short Equity	Convertible Hedging	Fixed-Income Hedging	General Hedging
3Q92	2.16	3.00	3.62	7.54	2.94
4Q92	2.27	2.70	3.07	6.65	3.19
1Q93	3.87	4.93	2.62	4.54	4.45
2Q93	2.95	4.73	2.68	7.87	6.78
3Q93	1.68	3.37	2.51	6.56	12.05
4Q93	1.85	4.85	2.90	4.39	5.24
1Q94	1.65	3.39	2.44	28.98	6.76
2Q94	2.00	3.09	3.08	4.29	8.08
3Q94	1.23	2.74	2.31	2.94	8.02
4Q94	2.43	2.89	2.90	2.91	8.80
1Q95	1.58	3.24	2.74	3.10	9.47
2Q95	1.89	3.02	2.81	10.98	4.13

when the size and number of mergers increased dramatically. By examining the cross-sectional standard deviations of quarterly returns, one can also see that the returns to the risk arbitrage managers in our universe are highly correlated. In other words, each individual manager's returns are close to the other manager's returns and, in general, resemble those of the average manager. Clearly, this is not to say that there are not exceptional risk arbitrage investment managers.

Conversely, the returns to the average long/short equity portfolio manager have the lowest average return during this time period. This might be attributable to the fact that, in this strategy's purest form, all the returns in this area are generated by an individual manager's skill. While there may be structural issues such as liquidity and complexity which may permit "excess" returns to generic strategies such as convertible bond hedging, there is no such opportunity in a long/short equity strategy where the stocks are highly liquid and heavily analyzed. When one compares the cross-sectional standard deviations to the average return, it is easy to see that there exists a moderate amount of variation in each manager's performance. For example, while the average manager was up 1.58 percent during the third quarter of 1993, approximately two-thirds of the managers returned between −1.42 percent and 4.58 percent. Moreover, slightly more than 15 percent of the investment managers earned more than 4.58 percent for the quarter. Unlike risk arbitrage, specific manager selection plays a much more important role in this area. Whereas in the risk arbitrage universe it is hard to find a manager who loses much on a frequent basis, this is not the case for the long/short equity portfolio strategy.

Convertible bond hedging has historically performed well with a good degree of consistency. Many attribute this phenomenon to the relative cheapness of convertible bonds as compared with the same firm's underlying equity or bonds. Rationales for the cheapness include relatively poor liquidity in many issues and the inherent complexity in the security design. By examining the cross-sectional data, one can see that, during the three-year period, the convertible bond managers had similar returns although they are not quite as correlated as the risk arbitrage managers.

Fixed-income hedging has also performed well although there is quite a lot of dispersion among the individual manager's returns. Clearly, this is an area where it makes a significant difference as to which investment manager one examines. One of the likely reasons for the large dispersion in fixed-income hedgers is that the portfolio composition and concentration vary enormously. For example, most convertible hedgers carry about 40 positions and there is often significant overlap in the types of positions held, while in fixed-income hedging there are several firms which have only five or six significant positions. Clearly, under this type of portfolio construction, one can experience significant volatility. When asked why these managers often have such concentrated portfolios, their answers usually involve the fact that they are trading the sovereign bonds swaps, and futures of G-7 nations, and, therefore, the number of investment opportunities at any one point are rather limited. For example, recently many firms have had an Italian bond position. While on the surface this may represent some investment similarity, it does not account for the fact that the managers do not tend to have the same positions. In other words, while many firms have only one Italian position, it is rarely structured in a similar way. Some invest in fixed-rate debt BTPs, others in the floating-rate CCTs, others use options, and so on. This dissimilarity and concentration among portfolios can be seen in the large variation in cross-sectional returns.

As mentioned earlier, the general arbitrage category contains two distinct types of investment managers. The predominant type is the generalist who engages in some combination of strategies and subsequently does not fit into just one universe. The other type of manager is the one who engages in a specialist strategy which does not fit one of the categories. Thus, it is not surprising that there tends to be a fair amount of dissimilarity among the managers contained in this universe as evidenced by the large cross-sectional standard deviations.

BUILDING A DIVERSIFIED
MARKET-NEUTRAL PORTFOLIO

Aggregating all the performance data provides some interesting observations. Figure 7–1 graphs the quarterly returns, net of fees, to our aggregate market-neutral universe. As can be seen, the universe as a whole tends to exhibit positive returns. The primary exception to this was the second quarter of 1994. Also, through time, the returns to the aggregate market-neutral universe have been relatively consistent.

Figure 7–2 graphs the quarterly returns in excess of Treasury bills for the aggregate market-neutral universe. Again, one can see that the universe as a whole, on a historical basis, has exhibited a fairly regular ability to outperform Treasury bills.[7]

Why are the universe returns so consistent, particularly when some of the substrategy composites produce negative returns on occasion? The answer lies in the low correlation among the many types of substrategies. The seven-year correlation coefficients for the various substrategies are as follows.

	Risk Arbitrage	Long/ Short	Convertible	Fixed-Income	General
Risk Arbitrage	1.00				
Long/ Short	0.04	1.00			
Convertible	0.16	0.21	1.00		
Fixed-Income	−0.07	0.18	0.30	1.00	
General	0.20	0.45	0.16	0.04	1.00

The low correlations among the various substrategies mean that a lower-risk portfolio of market-neutral strategies can be built by combining investments in these various substyles. The expected risk reduction is a function of

---

7. While there does exist a sample selection bias in the universe statistics because it is difficult to get the return data for poorly performing managers, we do try to reduce its impact through our selection criterion. See footnote 5.

Quarterly Performance of the Aggregate Market-Neutral Universe: 4Q85–3Q95

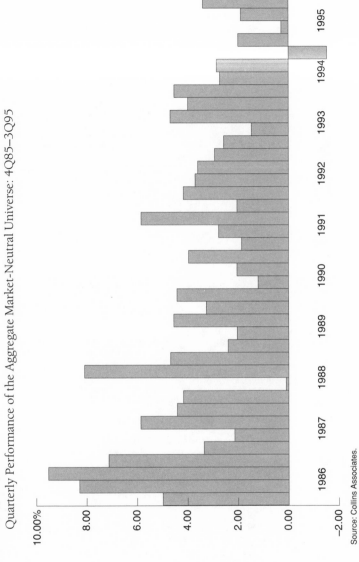

Source: Collins Associates.

FIGURE 7-2

Quarterly Performance of Aggregate Market-Neutral Universe Net of Treasury Bills: 4Q85–3Q95

Source: Collins Associates

118

the expected standard deviation for each style and its correlation with other styles. Historical data can be used as a guide, although we would not recommend using past performance as the sole basis for any investment decision.

CONCLUSION

There are many different styles of market-neutral investing including risk arbitrage, long/short equity portfolios, convertible bond hedging, and fixed-income hedging. While all these styles share the same basic approach, investing in one or more mispriced securities and hedging out the market risk, the styles tend to be relatively uncorrelated. In addition, within each style there can be quite a range in both method of implementation (i.e., leverage and portfolio composition) and realized performance. Nevertheless, a diverse portfolio of market-neutral styles has exhibited, on a historical basis, the ability to add value while reducing the risk to any one individual manager or strategy.

8

⑥ FUNDS OF FUNDS

Martin J. Gross
President
Sandalwood Securities, Inc.

It was only a matter of time before money managers found the Holy Grail, an investment strategy that could ply its trade by providing mid-teen annual returns with minimal monthly volatility, regardless of the direction of the equity and/or debt markets, or other traditional asset classes. So claimed numerous practioners of this market-neutral phenomenon. In fact, no sooner had many of these market-neutral funds opened their doors than institutional investors flooded them with capital. Unfortunately, 1994 was a traumatic year for many market neutral strategies. Many of these presumably lower-risk strategies incurred substantial unexpected losses, with some, like the Granite funds,[1] disappearing from the scene altogether. What went wrong here? Why was this supposed to be an attractive strategy and why did market-neutral funds like Askin &

---

1. In February and March of 1994, market-neutral funds operated by David Askin, which invested in mortgage-backed securities imploded causing losses estimated at in excess of $400 million. Shortly thereafter, the funds sought protection under the bankruptcy laws. An investigation surrounding their collapse is currently in process, with special focus on the conduct of the broker-dealers.

Fenchurch attract so much institutional capital, the former suffering in 1994, the latter in 1995?

The attraction of market-neutral investing was supported by a risk-return model employed by numerous consultants and other advisors. This highly quantitative model essentially equated risk with the volatility of historic returns. Analyzing the purchase of securities, especially equities, or the basic components of an investment strategy from a fundamental business risk perspective was secondary. Ignored were the potential benefits to volatility which allowed good business to be purchased at cheap prices due to short-term market fluctuations. Further, this model assumed that, of two strategies which each returned 15 percent per year over a certain defined time frame, the 15-percent return with the least volatility was preferable on a going-forward basis as the optimal risk-adjusted bet. The model also assumed that the time frame used as a measuring experience would be of sufficient duration to capture the relevant investment characteristics of that strategy under all market conditions to which the strategy could be subject. This qualitative premise assumed that future markets would not materially deviate from previous ones, and that past correlations between certain specific securities would remain relatively constant.[2] Minimal, if any, focus was given to whether these strategies represented good businesses on a going-forward basis in which to invest.

It was into this mind set that the market-neutral strategies, with their promised mid-teen returns (which significantly exceeded the historic returns on the S&P 500)[3] and

---

2. The collapse of the Granite funds was, at least in part, brought about by severe liquidity problems in the $1 trillion plus mortgage-backed securities (MBS) market which had never been previously experienced. In addition, the market-neutral strategy relied on bullish and bearish bonds being negatively correlated to each other. When both bullish and bearish bonds dropped at the same time, this sealed the fund's fate. Until it's demise, the size of the MBS market was thought sufficient to ensure its liquidity.

3. According to figures compiled by Ibottson Associates, the S&P 500 has compounded at an annual rate of 10 percent since 1926.

minimal volatility, as measured by their standard deviation, sold their wares. Market-neutral strategies promised good absolute return with less risk and, as if that weren't enough, a strategy that (at least in theory) was not affected by, or significantly correlated to, other traditional asset classes.

Armed with an accepted risk-return model and lulled to sleep by the label market neutral, these ventures set sail. As 1994 demonstrated, many of America's largest institutions which invested in market-neutral funds failed to penetrate into the specific characteristics of both the securities and the strategies these funds utilized. Since the track record fit the model, and the label "market neutral" reinforced both,[4] too few investors probed deeply into the specifics of these strategies. Colored extrapolation of past performance filled investors' computer screens as past returns, correlations, and minimal volatility were blindly assumed to go on *ad infinitum*.

I have adopted, for purposes of this chapter, David A. White's description of the universe of market-neutral strategies in the introduction to this book. Rather than narrowly defining market neutral, he observes that "the range of asset classes in which market-neutral strategies have been developed includes equities, convertible securities, high-yield bonds, fixed-income securities, currencies, and other asset classes."

This is instructive since it frees market-neutral investing from specific asset class parameters and shifts the focus

---

4. Many of the blind adherents of market-neutral strategies failed to heed the warning of the eighteenth century philosopher George Berkeley who, in his *Principles of Human Knowledge,* stated,

> It were, therefore, to be wished that everyone would use his utmost endeavors to obtain a clear view of the ideas he would consider, separating from them all that dress and encumbrance of words which so much contribute to blind the judgment and divide the attention . . . —we need only draw the curtain of words, to behold the fairest tree of knowledge, whose fruit is excellent and within the reach of our hand . . . Unless we take care to clear the first principles of knowledge from the embarrassment and delusion of words, we may make infinite reasonings upon them to no purpose; we may draw consequences from consequences, and be never the wiser.

to a methodology of risk reduction. White also notes that, in their quest for lower risk, the strategies make extensive use of leverage, derivatives, and highly complex portfolio structures to achieve their goals—an interesting contrast to say the least.

This chapter will review the concept of market neutral, analyze its applicability to funds of funds, and discuss whether funds of funds can achieve market neutrality without using any market-neutral strategies.

GENERAL TYPES OF FUNDS OF FUNDS

What are funds of funds? They are limited partnerships formed under state law.[5] Like hedge funds, they are limited to 99 investors, can't advertise, and are usually limited to "accredited investors." They do not make direct investments but allocate their capital to hedge funds. Unlike hedge funds, most funds of funds do not charge performance fees. The following chart is representative of the process.

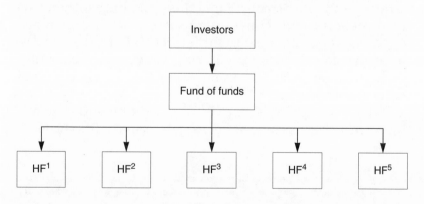

As investors in underlying hedge funds, a fund of funds' investment characteristics will reflect the strategies of the underlying recipients of its capital. As allocator, the general partner of the fund of funds will formulate

---

5. In general, funds of funds are limited partnerships, with a few organized as collective trusts. Most offshore funds of funds are corporations, with banks or other financial institutions serving as offshore administrators.

a strategy or investment orientation for the fund of funds, select those hedge funds to best implement that strategy, and monitor them on an ongoing basis.[6]

In Chapter 7 of *Hedge Funds,* a distinction was made among four basic types of funds of funds—target return, maximum return, dedicated strategy, or combinations of the above. Market-neutral funds of funds are best classified as target-return funds of funds since, in practice, most market-neutral hedge funds (and the funds of funds who use them exclusively) aim at 10-percent to 15-percent return.[7] They should not be considered dedicated strategy funds since differing strategies can produce a market-neutral effect, as we shall see.

Funds of Funds Limited to Market-Neutral Strategies

Funds of funds can be described as market neutral in a number of ways. First, and most simplistically, a market-neutral fund of funds can be one which allocates its capital to exclusively market-neutral strategies. The following chart would be representative of that process.

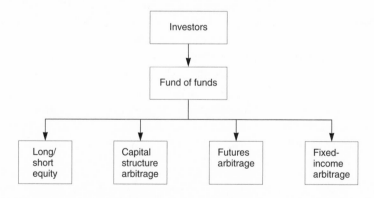

---

6. For a more complete treatment of funds of funds, see Jess Lederman and Robert A. Klein, eds., *Hedge Funds* (Burr Ridge, IL: Irwin, 1995), 85–101.

7. Target-return funds have a particular stated investment goal; maximum-return funds seek the best return under current market conditions, and often contain leveraged macro on other bets; dedicated-strategy funds focus on emerging markets, distressed securities, or long/short hedge funds, etc; and combination funds employ characteristics of the above types.

While a number of these funds of funds using only market-neutral strategies exist, most are not of this type.

The second and more interesting description of funds of funds as market neutral consists in the ability of a fund of funds manager to design a portfolio whose track record, consisting of the blended returns of the underlying hedge funds, bears no significant correlation to any traditional asset class. Would, or should, this count as a market-neutral fund of funds? This requires determining what it is about market-neutral strategies which makes them attractive investment options. Further, in spite of there being no commonly accepted definition of market neutral, it does require an examination of those characteristics market-neutral strategies in fact share.

Three basic ideas are embedded in the term market neutral, some explicit, others implicit. The first (explicit) assumes that the strategy will not be correlated to the equity and/or debt market, or any other traditional asset class, hence the neutrality. The second (implicit) assumes some minimal absolute return, either in excess of Treasury bills or over the historic return on the S&P 500. Absent a return in excess of some agreed-upon benchmark, the strategy would have no appeal. Third, also implicit, is that while there is no commonly agreed-upon volatility parameter that market-neutral funds must satisfy, a volatility clearly less than the S&P 500 is assumed. As White notes, investors in market-neutral strategies do not anticipate substantial volatility; quite the contrary.[8] In fact, while most market-neutral strategies have demonstrated low volatility, others have experienced sub-

---

8. Nothing in the term market neutral implies a low volatility. A completely uncorrelated (market-neutral) strategy could exhibit severe volatility on a monthly basis and yet be market neutral by virtue of a total lack of correlation to any market.

stantial losses, such as Granite in 1994 and Fenchurch in 1995. Granite showed, among other things, that lack of market correlation and low volatility do not always go hand in hand.[9]

Based on these three basic ideas embraced by market-neutral investing, a fund of funds which provided absolute monthly returns with low volatility and minimal correlation to the S&P 500 would appear to have the same essential return characteristics as a market-neutral fund of funds. Thus, it should not matter if the underlying strategies were market neutral but rather consisted of, for example, low-risk event-driven distressed securities and merger arbitrage strategies. In fact, they would be preferable to market-neutral strategies if they provided higher return with relatively similar volatility and lack of correlation to other traditional asset classes. Further, their lack of leverage, derivatives, and much-less-complex trading strategies reduce the effects manager risk can have on their portfolios.

Examples of Funds of Funds

Consider the example of two funds of funds, shown in Figures 8–1 and 8–2.[10] Both portfolios are constructed assuming no withdrawals. The market-independent portfolio consists of five highly regarded market-neutral managers, and the event-driven portfolio consists of six excellent event-driven managers. Audited monthly net returns are used for each fund.

---

9. Granite and Fenchurch used derivatives and leverage as part of highly complex strategies. Manager risk is all the greater, and less forgiving, under these circumstances.

10. Thanks are extended to Blaine Tomlinson of Financial Risk Management and his staff for assistance in creating the two test portfolios.

FIGURE 8–1

Monthly Returns for Market-Neutral Portfolio

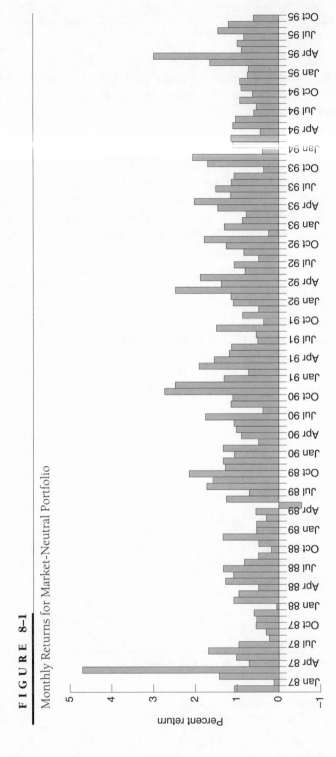

FIGURE 8-2

Monthly Returns for Event-Driven Portfolio

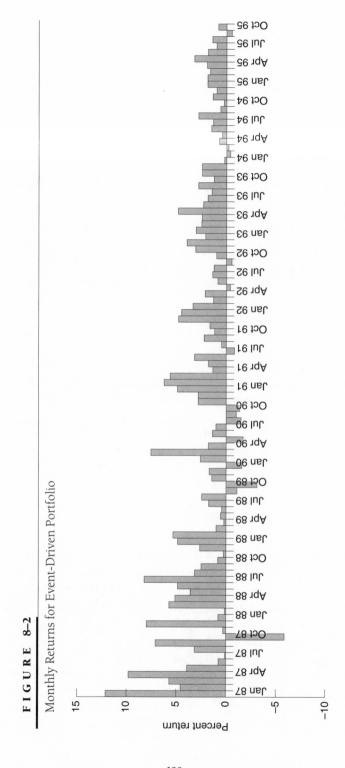

Various comparisons between the two portfolios are quite noteworthy:

	Portfolio Market Neutral	Portfolio Event Driven
Return analysis		
Total period return	224.17%	700.57%
Annualized geometric return	14.10	26.27
Average 12-month rolling return	13.88	24.63
Best 12-month rolling return	19.45	59.93
Worst 12-month rolling return	7.00	4.62
Consistency analysis		
Percent of up months	99.07%	84.11%
Percent of up 12-month rolling returns	100.00	100.00
Annualized standard deviation	2.68	11.10
Standard deviation of 12-month returns	2.95	12.33
Risk/downside analysis		
Annualized downside deviation (RF)	0.57%	3.32%
Largest drawdown	0.56	5.81
Average of largest 5 drawdowns	0.11	3.28

Both portfolios exhibit quite consistent characteristics as concerns percent of up months, 99.07 percent and 84.11 percent; percent of up 12-month rolling returns, each 100%; and standard deviation of 12-month returns, 2.95 percent and 12.33 percent. While the event-driven has higher drawdowns and annualized standard deviations, they are both relatively low. Perhaps most important, the event-driven portfolio provided a substantially higher return.

In reviewing quantitative data, qualitative factors always play a critical interpretive function. For example, while the comparisons choose top-performing funds in each sector, there was more risk in choosing a market-neutral fund in the last few years than an event-driven one in the distressed securities or merger arbitrage area. The blowups like Granite and, to a lesser extent, Fenchurch were in the market-neutral sector. In addition to Granite and Fenchurch, numerous convertible arbitrage market-neutral funds lost over 20 percent in 1994, while few, if

any, of the event-driven funds experienced similar problems over this period.

CONCLUSION

Market-neutral investing is characterized by return characteristics and investment methodology, not asset class. The
three ideal characteristics of market-neutral returns are

1. Minimal absolute return against a benchmark,
   such as Treasuries or the S&P 500;
2. Lack of correlation to the debt and/or equity
   market, and other traditional asset classes; and
3. Minimal volatility due to very hedged portfolio
   structures.

The market-neutral investment methodology is characterized by employment of substantial leverage, use of derivatives, and highly complex trading/investment strategies.
This combination of derivatives and leverage has resulted
in substantial losses in this sector in recent years, showing
that leverage increases risk, no matter how well-intended
the attempt to hedge. This use of leverage also clearly mag-
nifies the consequences of manager risk.

Funds of funds using driven distressed securities and
merger arbitrage strategies can generate good absolute returns with low volatility and a lack of correlation to other
traditional asset classes. And, since those strategies have
both avoided the blowups experienced by market-neutral
managers and provided significantly higher absolute returns with modest volatility and minimal correlation to
the equity and/or debt markets, and other traditional asset
classes, they provide a more attractive investment option
while retaining many of the anticipated benefits of market-
neutral strategies.

CHAPTER

9

⑥ INTERNATIONAL EQUITY MARKET-NEUTRAL STRATEGIES

Peter Swank, Ph.D.
Associate Director

David Krider
Associate
First Quadrant Corporation

From January 1980 to May 1995, the average proportion of stocks listed on the New York Stock Exchange having *positive* monthly returns was 52.6 percent. The immediate (and obvious) corollary: the average proportion of stocks having *nonpositive* monthly returns was 47.4 percent. The magnitude of the latter figure is quite remarkable.

Market-neutral, or, less restrictively, long/short equity investing is a strategy seeking to capitalize on this phenomenon. By selling short stocks with negative predicted return and buying stocks with a more-promising future, one can profit from market inefficiences in both directions.[1] There are several variations on this common theme, two of which are value neutral and market neutral. A value-neutral strategy is the less restrictive of the two, the only

---

1. A brief summary of arguments made in support of short-side inefficiencies in the U.S. equity market is presented in Bruce Jacobs and Kenneth Levy, "Long/Short Equity Investing," *Journal of Portfolio Management*, Fall 1993. However, all points made there carry over to the international equity markets discussed here.

restraint being that net investment must be zero at all times. A market- (or beta) neutral strategy imposes the additional constraint that the portfolio's covariance with the market must be zero. The restrictions imposed in the construction of the portfolio affect performance and return characteristics.[2]

This chapter extends the scope of analysis of market-neutral investing to several international equity markets. The country selection criteria for inclusion in this chapter were based solely on our investment experience: First Quadrant currently manages market-neutral equity portfolios in Japan and the United Kingdom, in addition to the United States. Canada would be a logical extension, and hence is an ongoing research interest.

A COMPARISON OF EQUITY RETURNS BEHAVIOR

The success of an investment strategy depends primarily on two factors:

- The process generating the asset returns in the investment universe under consideration; and

- The investment professional's ability to forecast accurately the risk and return characteristics of that process.

In this section we summarize some of the more salient equity returns characteristics that would affect the success of a long/short strategy, and compare them across the countries of interest. The underlying motivation for this exercise is that, while the behavior of equity returns varies to

---

2. The standard reference for equity market-neutral strategies is Bruce Jacobs and Kenneth Levy, op cit. A lively debate regarding the relative costs and benefts of market-neutral stategies is detailed in the following papers: Richard Michaud, "Are Long-Short Equity Strategies Reassessed," *Financial Analysts Journal,* September–October 1994; Bruce Jacobs and Kenneth Levy, "More on Long-Short Strategies," *Financial Analysts Journal,* March–April 1995.

some degree across markets, the key elements that would make for a successful long/short strategy are surprisingly similar.

Monthly Returns Proportions

In the introduction we noted that the the average proportion of stocks listed on the New York Stock Exchange with negative monthly returns was 47.4 percent. This fact suggests that the potential universe of profitably shortable stocks in the United States is indeed, on average, very large. This result applies to the other markets under consideration as well,[3] and is shown in Figures 9–1 through 9–4.

FIGURE 9-1

Canada:Proportion of Stocks with Positive Returns

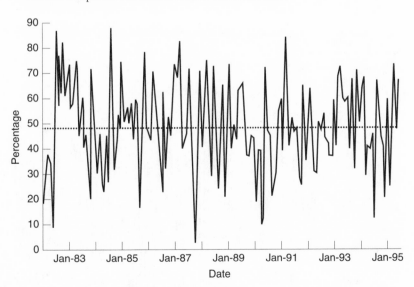

---

3. Average negative monthly proportions for the sample period were: Canada 51.0%, Japan 51.6%, and U.K. 46.0%.

FIGURE 9–2

Japan: Proportion of Stocks with Positive Returns

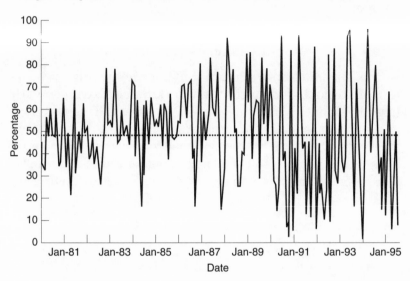

FIGURE 9–3

United Kingdom: Proportion of Stocks with Positive Returns

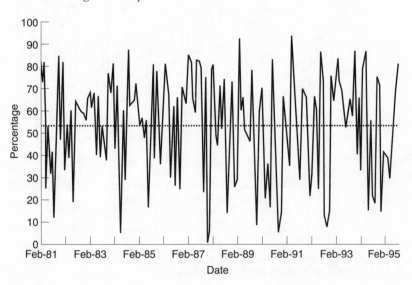

F I G U R E   9-4

United States: Proportion of Stocks with Positive Returns

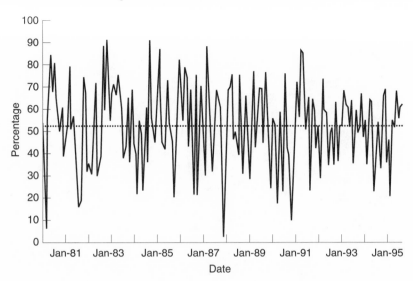

While it might be argued that the variability in proportions impinges on the successful implementation of a market-neutral strategy because a set of losing stocks this month become winners next month, the same problem exists with a long-only strategy.

Table 9-1 summarizes the sample statistics for monthly total returns for the constituents of the equity markets under consideration[4] for all returns, and for the conditional cases where there are positive returns only and negative returns only. While there are differences across markets for the aggregated returns case,[5] there is strong

---

4. See the Appendix to this chapter for details regarding data ranges and market indexes.
5. The differences may be exaggerated due to differences in survivorship bias across markets.

TABLE 9-1

Distributional Characteristics of Positive and Negative Returns

	Both	Positive	Negative
Canada			
Average	0.67	8.40	-7.52
Standard deviation	10.93	8.74	7.18
Japan			
Average	0.97	8.81	-6.74
Standard deviation	11.08	9.95	5.95
United Kingdom			
Average	1.48	7.94	-6.76
Standard deviation	10.14	7.86	6.93
United States			
Average	1.33	8.65	-7.41
Standard deviation	13.38	13.58	7.21

homogeneity in both means and standard deviations for the conditional cases.

Having even moderate ability to discriminate *a priori* between stocks with positive returns and those with negative returns would appear to be very profitable, given the magnitude of the sample means for the conditional cases.

Runs Behavior

In order to measure the degree of persistence, or inertia, in monthly returns, we calculate the relative frequency of sequences ("runs") of signed returns of a given length. The greater the frequency of runs of longer lengths, the greater is the tendency for winners (and losers) to repeat, and hence the greater is the degree of persistence in returns. Table 9-2 summarizes the positive and negative runs

TABLE 9-2

Positive and Negative Runs in Monthly Equity Returns

	Canada		Japan		United Kingdom		United States	
Length	Positive	Negative	Positive	Negative	Positive	Negative	Positive	Negative
1	23.75	27.82	26.57	23.80	22.51	26.46	23.83	26.16
2	12.55	12.08	12.46	12.90	12.78	12.56	12.44	12.55
3	5.82	5.73	5.85	6.76	6.90	6.23	6.26	6.02
4	3.07	2.63	2.79	3.77	3.17	2.83	3.34	2.90
5	1.77	1.18	1.26	1.28	1.75	1.33	1.91	1.30
6	1.08	0.48	0.71	0.80	1.01	0.55	0.98	0.58
7	0.62	0.19	0.33	0.25	0.57	0.28	0.52	0.28
8	0.44	0.13	0.14	0.10	0.32	0.11	0.29	0.13
9	0.23	0.07	0.06	0.06	0.24	0.07	0.16	0.08
10	0.12	0.02	0.03	0.02	0.16	0.03	0.07	0.05
11	0.09	0.01	0.01	0.02	0.04	0.01	0.05	0.02
12	0.05	0.01	0.01	0.00	0.05	0.01	0.03	0.01
13	0.01	0.00	0.01	0.00	0.01	0.00	0.01	0.01
14	0.02	0.00	0.00	0.00	0.01	0.00	0.01	0.00
15	0.01	0.00	0.00	0.00	0.00	0.00	0.00	0.00
16	0.00	0.00	0.00	0.00	0.00	0.00	0.00	0.00

behavior for the markets under consideration.[6] There is a tendency in all countries, with the exception of Japan, for positive runs to be of slightly longer length; in Japan, the opposite is true. Also, with the slight exception of Japan, the distribution of positive and negative runs is remarkably similar—the persistence of returns is almost identical across equity markets.[7]

Industry Runs Behavior

The slight asymmetry in positive versus negative run lengths is exaggerated when looking at industry runs behavior, both in the case of equally weighted industry returns (Table 9–3) and market capitalization-weighted industry returns (Table 9–4). In both cases, the tendency for persistence in industry returns is much stronger for winners than for losers, although the pattern of runs is very similar across markets, especially in the equally weighted returns case.

INSTITUTIONAL DETAILS

In the United States and many international markets, a long/short strategy is maintained through a prime brokerage arrangement. Responsibilities of a prime broker include

- Clearing and settlement of trades
- Custody
- Financing

---

6. The sequences were calculated for all names appearing at any time in the index detailed in the Appendix. All potentially incomplete sequences were excluded from the calculations.
7. It follows that the average run lengths for positive and negative runs are the same across markets: the average positive run length is incrementally greater than two, and average negative run length is incrementally less than two, with the exact opposite result for Japan.

TABLE 9-3

Positive and Negative Runs in Monthly Equal-Weighted Industry Returns

Length	Canada		Japan		United Kingdom		United States	
	Positive	Negative	Positive	Negative	Positive	Negative	Positive	Negative
1	22.07	27.35	21.51	25.86	17.40	29.10	18.90	27.80
2	11.97	10.57	12.36	11.34	13.37	11.56	12.98	12.05
3	5.56	5.75	6.41	6.38	7.46	6.36	6.13	5.95
4	3.61	2.95	3.24	4.22	3.39	2.18	3.20	3.18
5	2.33	1.71	1.48	0.83	2.00	0.79	2.52	1.15
6	1.28	0.82	1.76	0.96	1.73	0.45	2.28	0.18
7	0.74	0.27	1.42	0.09	0.90	0.11	1.08	0.05
8	0.97	0.08	0.62	0.09	0.87	0.08	1.08	0.07
9	0.47	0.31	0.65	0.03	0.38	0.00	0.50	0.02
10	0.08	0.00	0.15	0.00	1.17	0.00	0.16	0.02
11	0.43	0.04	0.22	0.00	0.19	0.00	0.29	0.00
12	0.27	0.00	0.19	0.00	0.34	0.00	0.16	0.00
13	0.27	0.00	0.06	0.00	0.11	0.00	0.16	0.00
14	0.00	0.00	0.06	0.00	0.08	0.00	0.07	0.00
15	0.08	0.00	0.00	0.00	0.00	0.00	0.05	0.00
16	0.00	0.00	0.00	0.00	0.00	0.00	0.00	0.00

TABLE 9-4

Positive and Negative Runs in Monthly Cap-Weighted Industry Returns

Length	Canada Positive	Canada Negative	Japan Positive	Japan Negative	United Kingdom Positive	United Kingdom Negative	United States Positive	United States Negative
1	20.49	29.03	21.67	27.42	17.76	30.68	17.57	30.12
2	13.47	10.08	13.42	11.99	13.74	13.13	13.57	11.78
3	5.86	5.82	6.38	5.72	7.33	4.59	6.13	5.64
4	3.32	2.76	3.45	3.05	3.35	1.71	4.03	2.21
5	2.13	1.49	1.84	0.83	2.10	0.39	2.66	0.44
6	1.94	0.45	1.15	0.55	1.46	0.07	2.21	0.16
7	0.86	0.22	0.89	0.20	0.93	0.04	1.06	0.11
8	0.90	0.04	0.58	0.00	1.00	0.00	1.02	0.00
9	0.37	0.00	0.32	0.06	0.53	0.00	0.53	0.00
10	0.15	0.00	0.12	0.00	0.68	0.00	0.18	0.00
11	0.34	0.00	0.12	0.00	0.14	0.00	0.27	0.00
12	0.11	0.00	0.06	0.00	0.32	0.00	0.13	0.00
13	0.08	0.00	0.03	0.00	0.00	0.00	0.07	0.00
14	0.00	0.00	0.00	0.00	0.04	0.00	0.09	0.00
15	0.04	0.00	0.00	0.00	0.04	0.00	0.00	0.00
16	0.08	0.00	0.00	0.00	0.00	0.00	0.02	0.00

- Provision of leverage
- Securities lending

Figure 9–5 provides a diagram of the central role that a prime broker plays in the implementation of the strategy. The process begins with the initial client funding, ¥50 billion for expositional purposes, and a determination of the list of attractive stocks to buy and unattractive stocks to short. After a small amount of the initial capital has been set aside for a liquidity buffer against potential changes in the short portfolio margin amount, the long portfolio is purchased with the remaining capital through an executing broker. Next, the prime broker must "source the shorts" and procure the borrowed stocks, which are then sold short by the executing broker.

Throughout this process there are several financing processes occurring. Collateral is required to be held against the borrowed stock accounts, and a small interest payment must be paid to the lenders of the shorted stock. As well, any dividend paid on the short portfolio must be

FIGURE 9–5

Role of the Prime Broker in Long/Short Strategy

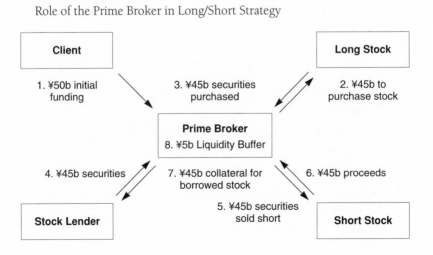

paid to the lenders. The collateral used for the short portfolio earns interest, known as the short rebate, as does the liquidity buffer. Any additional funds supplied by the prime broker in order to increase the degree of leverage of the portfolio incur interest, generally at a rate similar to the short rebate.

Unfortunately, there exists no "unified field theory" of international equity portfolio implementation, and local regulations and customs dictate certain deviations from the previous outline. We shall review some of these deviations for the countries in which we have experience.

United Kingdom

Market regulations in the United Kingdom restrict short sales of stock to registered market makers only. This restriction would ordinarily kill off any hopes of a market-neutral strategy; however, U.K. brokers have managed to circumvent this restriction by offering an OTC swap product which mimics the returns to a short security, without the necessity of dealing in the physicals market. This product, known as a contract for differences, is now widely available through leading U.K. brokerage houses, and has performance results which are only slightly different from those obtainable in the physicals market, if the latter were available.

Some of the benefits of these contracts include

- A separate, open-ended contract for each name in the portfolio
- A means of avoiding the 50 basis-point stamp tax on buys
- Daily marks-to-market
- A pricing mechanism linked directly to the physicals market
- Wide availability

Some of the drawbacks include

- A monopoly arrangement for the broker issuing the contract, since the contracts are not traded across brokerages
- Future availability subject to the whims of U.K. regulators, especially since a long-only version's primary benefit seems to be circumvention of the aforementioned stamp tax
- Liquidity and size constraints, due to their OTC nature

Japan

There are two primary obstacles with respect to managing Japanese market-neutral portfolios, which to a certain extent affect all non-U.K. countries: stock callability, and the issue of leverage.

Callability

Stock sold short, since it is still the property of another investor, may be recalled by the owner at any time for any reason. While this is a problem for a portfolio in any country, it is especially dire for Japanese portfolios. Japanese investors, for reasons tied to *keiretsu* custom, like to be owners of record for voting purposes. As a result, they will call back loaned stock for the record date. Since dividends are paid semiannually, this phenomenon occurs semiannually as well. If there were no other source of borrowable stock, the ability to run a market-neutral strategy would be severely constrained, and portfolios would have to be liquidated on a very regular basis. Fortunately, U.S. index funds provide a relatively large and stable pool of borrowable stock that is free of the callability feature. Note the obvious oxymoron that noncallable stock is still callable; short portfolio holdings can be called away on occasion.

Leverage

In U. S. long-short programs, long securities are generally used to satisfy the margin requirements of the securities sold short. The Federal Reserve Board, through its Regulation "T," has approved, for margining purposes, certain foreign securities that meet its requirements. If a long portion of a market-neutral portfolio holds a sufficiently large number of non-Regulation "T" stocks, its ability to finance the short portion of the portfolio will be greatly diminished. In addition, the ability of prime brokers to extend leverage will be dependent on the marginability of the long portfolio.

PERFORMANCE: LIVE AND SIMULATED

The theoretical advantages ascribed to market-neutral strategies translate well into superior performance, both live and in simulation. Table 9–5 details the return and risk profiles for the simulated returns in each of the strategies.[8] Simulated returns are net of transactions costs and have been reduced by 33 percent to account for the upward bias generally observed in simulated portfolio returns. All figures are reported in the currency local to that country. The simulations perform above their respective benchmarks in all three countries while still maintaining an acceptable level of variance. With an active return/risk ratio of 1.75, the simulations in Japan performed exceedingly well.

The simulated returns are generated from portfolios backtested using historical returns data. A simulation begins with a portfolio consisting entirely of cash, which is then rebalanced to reflect our forecasted alpha. This process is repeated on a monthly basis to emulate the actual rebalancing process that would be used under live

---

8. Simulated performance is not a guarantee of future returns.

TABLE 9-5

Return and Risk for Simulated Portfolios
February 1987 through August 1995

	United Kingdom			Japan			United States		
	T-Bill	Market Neutral	Value Added	T-Bill	Market Neutral	Value Added	T-Bill	Market Neutral	Value Added
Average monthly return	0.75	1.52	0.78	0.37	1.30	0.93	0.46	1.00	0.54
Annualized cumulative return	9.34	19.59	10.24	4.49	16.36	11.87	5.64	12.44	6.81
Annual standard deviation	0.85	7.38	7.33	0.55	7.83	7.81	0.54	5.68	5.64
Return/risk	11.03	2.65	1.40	8.21	2.09	1.52	10.42	2.19	1.21

TABLE 9–6

Return and Risk for Live Portfolios

	United Kingdom April 1994—Aug 1995			United States June 1991—Aug 1995		
	T-Bill	Market Neutral	Value Added	T-Bill	Market Neutral	Value Added
Average monthly return	0.49	0.72	0.23	0.33	0.85	0.52
Annualized cumulative return	6.03	8.91	2.88	4.03	10.49	6.46
Annual standard deviation	0.35	4.25	4.33	0.31	5.74	5.69
Return/risk	17.26	2.09	0.66	12.80	1.83	1.14

conditions. Transactions costs are computed from average portfolio turnover and the direct expenses associated with rebalancing.

Table 9–6 contains comparable data for live returns. The market-neutral strategy in the United Kingdom has been "live" for 17 months. In the United States it has been trading for over four years. Japan is omitted from this analysis because its short trading history (two months) would not yield a statistically strong indication of the strategy's viability.[9] The market-neutral portfolios in both countries have significantly outperformed their benchmarks with an active return/risk ratio of 1.14 in the United States and 0.66 in the United Kingdom.

The analysis for Japan and the United Kingdom changes slightly when currency effects are taken into consideration. Failing to hedge out currency risk increases the

---

9. Over these two months it has performed 34 percent (annualized) in excess of its benchmark, the Japanese equivalent of the U.S. T-bill.

TABLE 9–7

Unhedged Return and Risk for International Portfolios,
Simulated and Live Returns Combined
February 1987 through August 1995

	United Kingdom			Japan		
	T-Bill	Market Neutral	Value Added	T-Bill	Market Neutral	Value Added
Average monthly return	0.84	1.76	0.92	0.87	1.79	0.92
Annualized cumulative return	9.70	22.05	12.35	10.14	22.55	12.41
Annual standard deviation	12.35	14.42	7.14	12.10	14.38	7.86
Return/risk	0.79	1.53	1.73	0.84	1.57	1.58

portfolios' volatility, as demonstrated in Table 9–7. Depending upon relative movements in the foreign exchange, the returns can either be enhanced or diminished as a result. It should be noted that the data in Table 9–7 were computed from a combination of simulated and live returns. Live returns were used when available, otherwise the simulated data were used to extend the returns history back to February 1987.

Hedging out currency risk incurs a cost. However, it reduces the risk of investing across national borders. The effect of hedging is illustrated in Table 9–8. Again, simulated returns were used when live returns were not available. Volatility is reduced through hedging, but it is not brought back to the level observed in returns calculated in the local currency for two reasons. First, the cost of hedging is related to the relative interest rates prevailing in the two countries. Second, the relevant benchmark for the two countries with currency hedging is now the U.S. T-Bill, which is less positively correlated with hedged returns in

TABLE 9-8

Hedged Return and Risk for International Portfolios,
Simulated and Live Returns Combined
February 1987 through August 1995

	United Kingdom			Japan		
	T-Bill	Market Neutral	Value Added	T-Bill	Market Neutral	Value Added
Average monthly return	0.46	1.37	0.92	0.46	1.38	0.92
Annualized cumulative return	5.64	17.53	11.89	5.64	17.54	11.90
Annual standard deviation	0.54	6.98	7.09	0.54	7.90	7.83
Return/risk	10.42	2.51	1.68	10.42	2.22	1.52

the two countries than the local currency returns are with their respective T-bill equivalents.

The following sections give a country-by-country breakdown of portfolio returns. Live and simulated returns are provided, as well as hedged and unhedged returns for the international portfolios.

The United States

The United States market-neutral portfolio has been actively traded since June 1991. As previously detailed in Table 9-5, it has outperformed its benchmark by 6.81 percent (annualized). Performance has been consistent, with positive active returns in 55 percent of the months and in 76% of the quarters. In simulation, active returns have also been positive and consistent. Figures 9-6 and 9-7 are graphs of the live and simulated performance respectively. An interesting feature may be noted in the period extending from April 1994 to August 1995, when returns seem to flatten out. Active portfolio management requires a volatile

FIGURE 9–6
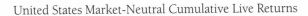

United States Market-Neutral Cumulative Live Returns

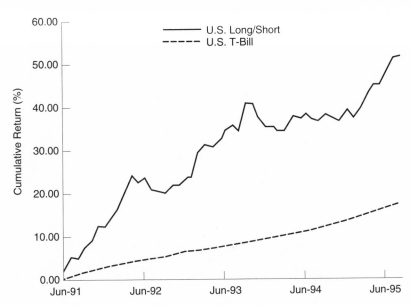

market in order to realize the gains due to timing its swings correctly. During the period in question, market volatility[10] was lower than at any previous period in the study. This phenomenon may be observed in the United Kingdom and, to a lesser extent, in Japan as well.

The United Kingdom

Active returns to the traded market-neutral portfolio in the United Kingdom are an impressive 10.24 percent. The active returns are also consistent, being positive in 63 percent of all months and in 60 percent of all quarters from April 1994 to August 1995. Figures 9–8 and 9–9 are graphs of the live and simulated performance respectively. Again, market volatility

10. As measured by a trailing 12-month standard deviation of returns to the S & P 500 index

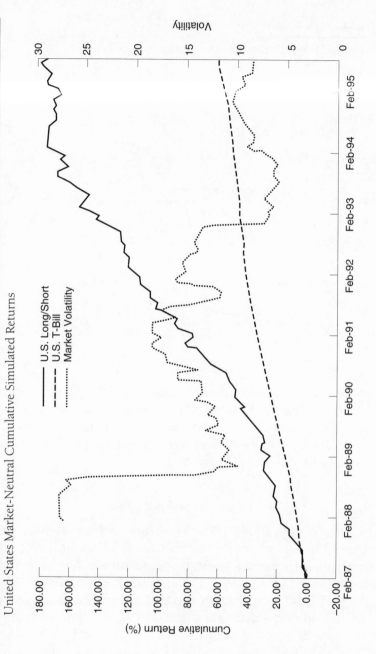

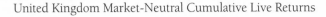

FIGURE 9–8

United Kingdom Market-Neutral Cumulative Live Returns

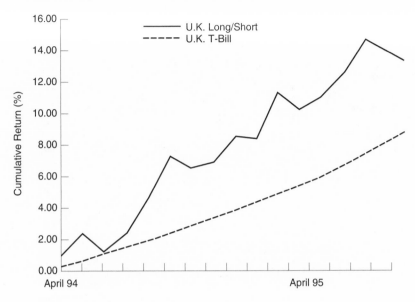

is plotted along with the simulated portfolio returns to illustrate the connection between swings in valuation and active performance. The two remaining graphs of U.K. performance illustrate the effect of currency hedging upon performance. In Figure 9–11, it is apparent that returns become much more volatile when exchange rate effects are taken into account. Hedging away currency risk will reduce this volatility substantially, as illustrated in Figure 9–10.

Japan

The Japanese market-neutral portfolio exhibits characteristics similar to those found in the U. S. and U. K. strategies. The connection between volatility and performance appears weaker in this country as seen in the graph of simulated performance found in Figure 9–12. Figures 9–13 and 9–14

FIGURE 9–9

United Kingdom Market-Neutral Cumulative Simulated Returns

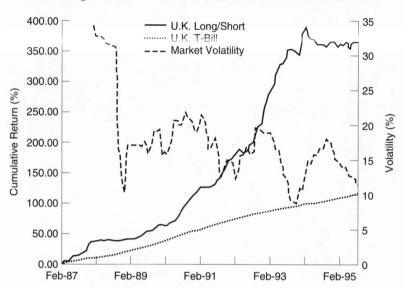

FIGURE 9–10

United Kingdom Market-Neutral Cumulative Hedged Returns

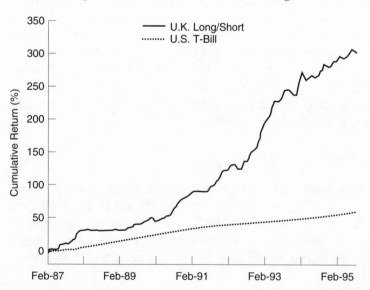

FIGURE 9–11

United Kingdom Market-Neutral Cumulative Unhedged Returns

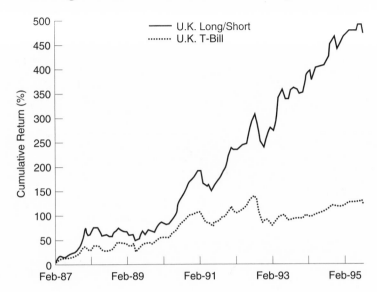

FIGURE 9–12

Japan Market-Neutral Cumulative Simulated Returns

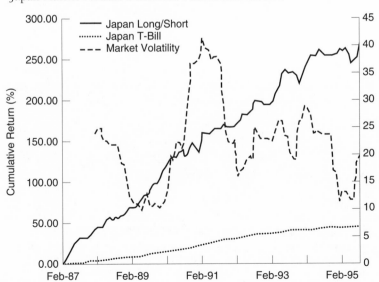

FIGURE 9–13

Japan Market-Neutral Cumulative Hedged Returns

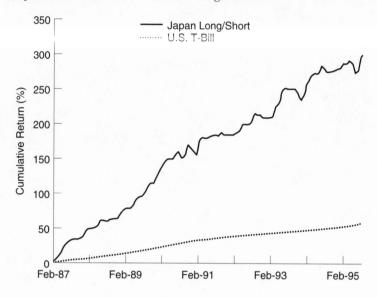

FIGURE 9–14

Japan Market-Neutral Cumulative Unhedged Returns

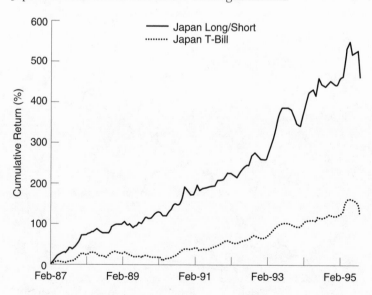

graph the hedged and unhedged cumulative returns respectively.

Canada

Although not included in the preceding analysis, Canada shows some theoretical promise as a candidate for market-neutral investment. Research into the viability of a Canadian market-neutral strategy is being pursued; however, practical considerations may hinder the implementation of such a portfolio. Figure 9–15 is a graph of simulated returns to such a portfolio. These returns have been reduced by 33 percent and are net of transactions costs to bring them in line with what may be expected in a comparable live portfolio.

F I G U R E   9–15

Canada Market-Neutral Cumulative Simulated Returns

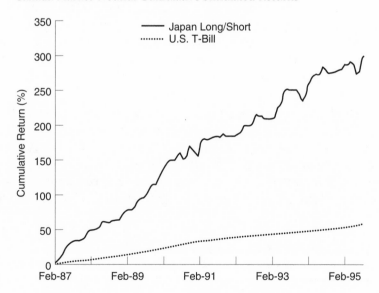

TABLE 9–9

Correlation between Hedged Market-Neutral Returns and the Market
for Each Country, Simulated and Live Returns Combined
February 1987 through August 1995

	Correlation
United Kingdom	0.03
Japan	0.37
United States	−0.26

BELLS AND WHISTLES

When the returns to a market-neutral portfolio are sufficiently uncorrelated with those of another portfolio, the
two may be combined into one overlay strategy. In this way,
the alpha due to both may effectively be added together.
Thus, the market-neutral active return can be considered
portable in the sense that it may be combined with a wide
range of other strategies. A simple strategy that takes advantage of this is that of the equity overlay, sometimes referred to as equitization. Table 9–9 demonstrates that the
correlations between the market-neutral portfolios and
their corresponding market proxies are fairly low over the
combined simulation and live histories.[11] Table 9–10 details the risk and return characteristics of the equity overlay. As expected, the active returns do not differ markedly
from those associated with the market-neutral portfolios
considered separately. The great benefit of the combined-
market/market-neutral overlay is in the reduced transactions costs. A traditional long portfolio allows active

---

11. The correlation for Japan is unusually high for a market-neutral portfolio.
    This is primarily due to unusual market conditions over the period under
    construction.

TABLE 9-10

Return and Risk for Hedged "Equitized" Portfolios, Simulated and Live Returns Combined
February 1987 through August 1995

	United Kingdom			Japan			United States		
	FTSE 100	Equity Overlay	Value Added	Topix Sect. 1	Equity Overlay	Value Added	S&P 500	Equity Overlay	Value Added
Average monthly return	0.87	1.79	0.92	0.16	1.08	0.92	1.05	1.63	0.58
Annualized cumulative return	9.07	21.31	12.24	−0.70	9.89	10.59	12.18	20.31	8.14
Annual standard deviation	18.33	19.82	7.09	23.05	26.98	7.83	14.38	13.97	5.80
Return/risk	0.49	1.07	1.73	−0.03	0.37	1.35	0.85	1.45	1.40

TABLE 9–11

Correlation of Hedged Returns across Countries,
Simulated and Live Returns Combined
February 1987 through August 1995

	United Kingdom	Japan	United States
United Kingdom	1.000	0.029	0.048
Japan	0.029	1.000	−0.090
United States	0.048	−0.090	1.000

FIGURE 9–16

Mean Variance Efficient Frontier, Fully Hedged

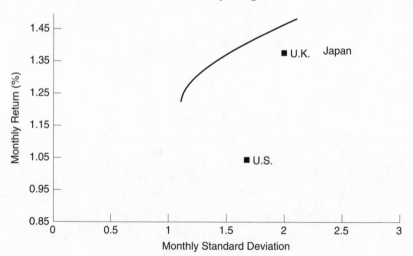

returns to be reduced by excessive transactions costs simply to "buy the market." In contrast, futures can be used to implement the market portion of the overlay strategy. The savings can be substantial.

Returns to market-neutral portfolios are noted for their lack of correlation across countries, as noted in Table 9–11. This would indicate that much of the systemic risk associated with a country's portfolio taken individually, can be diversified away when held jointly with those portfolios associated with the other countries. In this way, the investor can move farther out on the mean-variance efficient frontier as illustrated in Figure 9–16. Note that none of the portfolios lies on the mean-variance efficient frontier. This implies that one is always better off holding a "portfolio of portfolios" rather than investing entirely in one of the countries.

CONCLUSION

There are a large number of poor equity investments. This should not come as a surprise to any seasoned investment professional. However, in traditional investing, the best a portfolio manager can do is to not own those stocks. This imposes a strict limitation on the bet he or she can make with his or her equity positions. In contrast, long/short investing more effectively capitalizes on this phenomenon by selling short those stocks with substantially negative expected returns. In this way, there is no ceiling to the possible bets one can make against a particular stock or market sector.

First Quadrant has been managing market-neutral portfolios for over four years. The countries in which we currently have trading portfolios are the United States, Japan, and the United Kingdom. All are performing substantially above their respective benchmarks, the U.S. T-bill or its equivalent, with tolerable risk. Through hedging, currency risks may be eliminated, greatly reducing volatility.

Provided the long/short portfolio is sufficiently uncorrelated with another portfolio, one may be overlain upon the other to provide a form of "portable alpha." We demonstrated this in the case of a market-neutral portfolio and a market-proxy portfolio. The active returns in simulation were substantially positive. If futures are used to buy into the market, then transactions costs are reduced by a wide margin.

Mathematical Details of Factors and the Optimization Process

Monthly equity total returns were graciously supplied by BARRA, Inc. The time-spans and universes for the countries under consideration were as follows:

- U.S.A.   1980:01—1995:05   NYSE
- U.K.   1981:01—1995:05   FT All Shares
- Japan   1980:01—1995:05   TOPIX
- Canada   1982:01—1995:05   TSE 300
- Mathematical Details of Factors and Optimization Process

Equity management at First Quadrant is based upon the BARRA model of factor returns. We assume that monthly stock excess returns are described by the following relation:

$$R_s - R_{rf} = \sum_f \beta_{sf} R_f + \tilde{\varepsilon}_s$$

where β_f are factor exposures, and R_f are the factor returns. BARRA estimates the factor exposures, which are *attributes* of the individual securities, and the factor returns which are *common* to all equities in the economy. Our models predict factor returns one time period (month) ahead.

$$R_f^{t+1} = f\left(X_i^t\right) + \tilde{\varepsilon}_f^{t+1}$$

where R_f^t is the factor return at time t, and the X_i^t are data publicly available at time t (these data may include lagged versions of the time series to be predicted). The function, f, that generates the factor forecasts is estimated using a proprietary process. When the data are made available, the models are reestimated and the forecasted factor returns along with our current equity positions are fed into a mean-variance optimizer which optimally rebalances the portfolio.

Let $\mathbf{x}$ be the vector composed of the universe of equity returns for the time interval $[t,t+T]$. Let $E[\mathbf{x}] = \mu$ and $Var[\mathbf{x}] = \mathbf{V}$ be the expected returns and variance-covariance matrix for $\mathbf{x}$, respectively. Define the vectors $\mathbf{b}$, $\mathbf{p}$, and $\mathbf{w}$ as the vector of weights associated with the benchmark portfolio, the managed portfolio, and the active portfolio, respectively. Note that $\mathbf{w} = \mathbf{p} - \mathbf{b}$.

Under mean-variance assumptions, the long-only portfolio optimization problem is to choose the vector of active weights $\mathbf{w}$:

$$\max_{\mathbf{w}} \mathbf{w'x} - \lambda\mathbf{w'Vw}$$

subject to

$\mathbf{w'}1 = 0$ (all active weights sum to zero)

$\mathbf{c}_1 \leq \mathbf{Mw} \leq \mathbf{c}_2$ (additional optimizer constraints)

Under mean-variance assumptions, the market-neutral-portfolio optimization problem is to choose the vector of active weights $\mathbf{w}$:

$$\max_{\mathbf{w}} \mathbf{w'x} - \lambda\mathbf{w'Vw}$$

subject to

$\mathbf{w'}1 = 0$

$Cov[\mathbf{w'x},\mathbf{b'x}] = 0$

$\mathbf{c}_1 \leq \mathbf{Mw} \leq \mathbf{c}_2$.

The optimizer gives a recommended trade list, which is then applied to the current portfolio. To backtest a strategy, the preceding process is repeated periodically from a base time-period to the present.

10

⑥ # DOMESTIC CUSTODIAL ISSUES

Jane E. Sinclair
Western Regional Director
Neuberger & Berman

The previous chapters in this book have made it clear that the common denominator for all types of market-neutral investing is the ability of the portfolio to short securities. In order to facilitate a short sale, the client/advisor must be able to borrow the securities until the position is covered by a buy transaction. The Federal Reserve Board regulations require short positions to be held in an account with a broker-dealer. The advisor must use a broker-dealer to borrow the securities on behalf of its clients, and the firm is designated the sub-custodian or prime broker in carrying the short positions.

PRIME BROKERAGE

Prime brokerage actually began in the 1950s with the notable A. W. Jones's trade requiring execution with one broker and settlement of the same trade with another broker, or prime broker. Prime brokerage clearing came to the forefront in the 1980s, providing investment advisors with the ability to execute with one or more registered broker-dealer(s), with settlement of all trades taking place in one common account held in the client's name at the prime broker. There are three parties to a prime broker transaction: the client or advisor on behalf of its clients, the prime broker, and the executing broker.

SEC No-Action Letter

The Securities and Exchange Commission (SEC), at the request of its prime broker committee[1], issued a no-action letter dated January 25, 1994, outlining the requirements to maintain a prime brokerage arrangement. Clients execute prime broker agreements which specify the terms of settling transactions executed away and cleared through the prime broker. This agreement also names all executing brokers intended to be used. The executing broker(s) receive a letter from the prime broker agreeing to clear and carry each trade placed by the client or its advisor.

Terms and Conditions

An account is opened on the books of the executing broker in the name of the prime broker for the benefit of the client (e.g., ABC Securities FOB The XYZ Retirement Trust). The tax identification number of the prime broker is used as well. This ensures proper notice of any trailing dividends or reorganization items should a trade be settled on a post-settlement-date basis. On trade date, the advisor notifies the prime broker of all trades completed by the executing broker(s). The trade is input into the client's account, and the prime broker has an offsetting trade in a "fail to receive/deliver" account with the executing broker. The prime broker issues a confirmation to the client and affirms the trade with the executing broker through the Depository Trust

---

1. The prime broker committee consisted of representatives from prime brokers, executing brokers, and the credit division of the securities industry association. See Douglas G. Preston, "SEC Issues No-Action Letter Regarding Prime Broker Arrangements," *Securities Industry Association Legal Alert #93-1,* February 7, 1994. See also, "SEC No-Action Letter Addressed to Prime Broker Committee," January 25, 1994 (Brandon Becker, Director).

FIGURE 10-1

Role of the Prime Broker

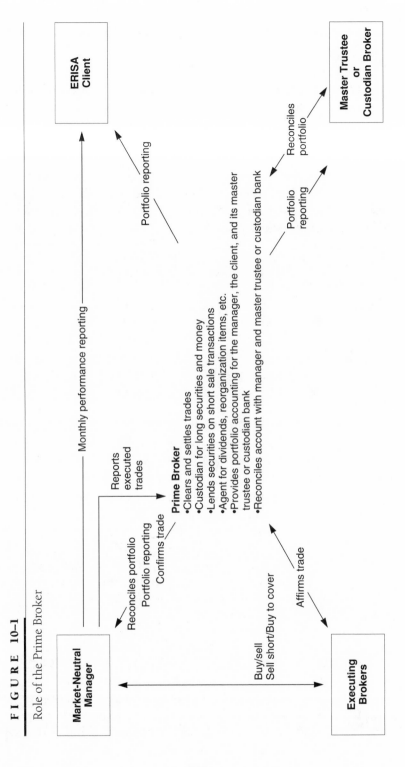

Company's institutional delivery system. Duplicate confirmations are sent to the advisor as well. Any trade differences are brought to the attention of the advisor on the morning of trade date plus one. The advisor notifies the prime broker of any corrections to the trade in order to make settlement with the executing broker. After affirming the trade with the executing broker, the trade is cleared and settled under normal settlement procedures of tradedate plus three business days.

Member Firm Requirements

The SEC requires that certain financial conditions be met by the broker-dealers involved in a prime broker arrangement. Minimum net capital requirements are $1,500,000 for prime brokers and $1,000,000 for executing brokers. Client accounts managed by an investment advisor registered under the Investment Advisors Act of 1940 must maintain a minimum equity of $100,000 in cash or securities. Strict attention should be given to the prime broker and executing brokers' net capital, and how the firm's capital is used. It is prudent of the advisor to review the financial statements of these firms periodically and request a statement of the safety and soundness as to the client's assets being held by the prime broker. The statement should address possession and control of client securities, internal audit procedures, and insurance coverage of accounts. The safekeeping of securities from loss or theft generate added concern by the advisor. An inquiry should be made into the firm's procedure for disaster recovery in the event of a power outage, a fire, or flood.

PENSION FUNDS AND TAX-EXEMPT INVESTORS

With the new ruling on short sales discussed in Chapter 2, the Internal Revenue Service has cleared the way for pension funds, endowments, and other tax-favored institutional investors to use investment strategies involving short sales of securities[2] such as market neutral. There are specific legal documents that dictate the terms and conditions and it is entered into by the following three parties: the client, usually represented by a master trustee or custodian bank ("client"), the investment advisor ("advisor"); and the subcustodian or prime broker ("custodian"). The term subcustodian is used when referring to the broker-dealer, who is considered subordinate to the master trustee or custodian bank.

REQUIRED DOCUMENTATION

The custodian agreement provides for the client's authorization of the advisor to invest assets on behalf of the client, with specific language governing short sales. The advisor is given exclusive authority over, and responsibility for, the investment management of assets and the directing of the custodian in the settlement of trades with brokers or others designated by the advisor. The agreement further authorizes the custodian to open an account in the client's name according to general brokerage practices and applicable laws under the Securities Exchange Act of 1934. All the terms of reporting transactions, collection of dividends on long purchases, disbursement of dividends on short sales, interest payments, and all other distributions received are included in this agreement. The custodian usually supplies this agreement; however, several master trustee banks now have their own document. All parties need to be flexible as to which agreement will be used. This agreement should be reviewed by legal counsel of all parties prior to execution.

The customer agreement is a standard brokerage document. An expanded form of this document is used for clients that would traditionally use a bank as their custodian. The customer agreement involves the same three par-

---

2. Vineeta Anand, "Pension Funds May Sell Short: IRS," *Pensions & Investments,* January 9, 1995.

ticipants as the custodian agreement. It provides for all terms and conditions under which the prime broker will maintain the client's account for purchases and sales of securities and other property, and any other related transactions. It binds all parties to applicable laws, rules, and regulations of all state, federal, and self-regulatory agencies such as the New York Stock Exchange and the Board of Governors of the Federal Reserve System, which specifies required payment for securities.

The customer agreement gives the prime broker all the rights and remedies available to a secured creditor should a client breach or default under the agreement. This agreement should be accompanied by the prime broker's truth-in-lending disclosure statement, which will outline any extension of credit. Specific language authorizes the prime broker to pledge the client's property, consisting of the proceeds from short sales, as collateral for securities borrowed by the prime broker on behalf of the account in order to effectuate short sales. The standard brokerage industry arbitration disclosures will also appear in this document. The customer agreement is supplied by the prime broker and should be reviewed by legal counsel of all parties prior to execution.

MARKET-NEUTRAL INVESTING

Long Portfolio

The account is initially funded with a wire of funds from the master trustee bank. Ninety to 95 percent of the initial funding will be invested in long securities. If the account is funded by a transfer of securities from a previous manager, the advisor may want to review the holdings and liquidate or cover those positions in the old portfolio. On funding date, only those securities that would work in the new universe of long buys would be received into the new account, plus the liquidated funds. The long securities are then used as collateral for an equal amount invested in short sales.

Short Portfolio

The investing in the short portfolio usually will take place simultaneously with the purchase of the longs. The executing broker has the responsibility of locating shares that will be available to borrow *prior* to effecting the client's short sale. The security should be available to borrow on behalf of the client no later than the settlement date. Since the trade will ultimately settle with the prime broker, the executing broker may look to the prime broker in locating these shares.

The advisor may wish to give the prime broker a sample short universe of the securities intended for short sale to determine availability. Lending agreements must be in place between the lender, which may be another broker-dealer or a bank on behalf of its institutional clients, and the borrower, which may be the executing broker or prime broker.

The prime broker has a stock loan department that continually maintains the proper loan to cover client short sales. Lenders may send notification requesting stock to be returned or stocks that are subject to buy-in because they have been sold by the lender and are needed for delivery. The stock loan department locates other shares with another lender, and the positions remains secure. This procedure takes place all day and is transparent to the client. Buy-ins may be processed on an allocated basis of the entire short-stock record on the prime broker's books, or it may take place on a last-in, first-out basis. The advisor should inquire regarding the prime broker's firm policy if the prime broker has not disclosed this information.

Collateralizing Short Sales

The lending institution will receive the proceeds of the client's short sale from the prime broker as collateral for securities borrowed. Remember, the client allows for this under the terms of the customer agreement. The prime broker may also use Treasury bills, but typically the proceeds of the short sale are used. If the price of the stock goes down, excess collateral is returned to the borrower. Conversely, when the stock goes up additional collateral is sent to the lender. This is known as marking to the market.

Rebate on Shorts

The lending institution pays the prime broker a rebate fee which is determined by the dollar amount or size and the quality of the securities borrowed. The prime broker pays a portion of this rebate fee to the client, also based upon the size and the quality of the short sales. The rebate rate is negotiated by the advisor and the prime broker, and may represent a percentage of the broker's call rate. The broker's call rate may differ slightly from the published Broker's Call Rate in *The Wall Street Journal* and from firm to firm. It is usually based upon the average rate of several major banks which lend to brokers. The rebate rate may also be based as a percentage of the federal funds rate or an equivalent to the 30-day Treasury bills.

If there are difficult-to-borrow securities at any time during the lending period, an adjustment in the rebate rate may be made for that period. The adjustment could be a lower rate paid, down to a zero rebate. Difficult-to-borrow securities occur when there is an interest by investors to short certain securities and the shares are not available to borrow. The difficult-to-borrow period may last a few days or indefinitely. *Barron's* publishes the open short-interest in stocks once a month. Market-neutral advisors do not typically have difficult-to-borrow securities in their short universe.

Cash Reserve

Market-neutral advisors usually allow for a cash reserve of 5 to 10 percent held in the account for marks to the market. This excess cash will earn interest daily on a rate that should be equivalent to the 30-day Treasury bill or current money market rates, accrued daily and paid monthly.

Hedging with the S&P 500 Index Futures

If you choose a market-neutral advisor that hedges the portfolio with the S&P 500 Index future, it would be efficient to use a prime broker that is also registered with the Commodity Futures Trading Commission (CFTC) as a futures commissions merchant. Futures transactions are governed by the CFTC in the same way securities transactions are governed by the SEC. Client futures positions and Treasury bills or funds used as collateral must be held in a separate account and may not be commingled with the client's securities account.

Futures transactions have one-day settlements and, therefore, the marks to the market are met daily by funds deposited for deficient margin requirements or funds paid out for excess requirements held. Using a master trustee or custodian bank may be cumbersome to meeting the daily marks. Each day, it would require someone from the prime broker calling the client's bank to wire funds or advise of funds being sent. Accounts could incur additional fees for the daily wire of funds. Most prime brokers have automated the movement of funds between the client's securities and futures accounts without any additional fees.

PORTFOLIO REPORTING

Beyond consolidated settlement of all transactions, wherever executed, most prime brokers provide portfolio accounting. This allows for daily reconciliation between the prime broker and the advisor. A separate report of all transactions, including dividends and reorganization items, should be available. Most advisors maintain a separate in-house portfolio system in order to reconcile with their custodians and prime brokers. Reports should be available for viewing on screen or in print format. The long portfolio and the short portfolio should be separate reports, with an overlay report combining balances, total liquid equity, and available investment cash.

At the end of the trading day, advisors should be able to input their trades directly, via personal computer, into the prime broker's client accounts. Some prime brokers have the capability of accepting a file from the advisor's own portfolio system, therefore allowing for one single entry of data and reducing the risk of error or duplication.[3]

The prime broker should interface via computer with the advisor and the master trustee bank. Electronic communication utilizing user-friendly systems is essential for efficient market-neutral investing. Most master trustee banks oversee the activities of the prime broker as a continuing service to their clients. Portfolio reporting should be easily accessible and have more than one application for sorting information to meet the needs of all parties. The advisor may need daily information, while the master trustee bank may want to see weekly or monthly reviews.

Historical data pertaining to the transactions in the portfolio should be available via computer access for the last 12 months, at a minimum. This may be essential for annual audits as well as mergers and acquisitions or reorganizations involving spin-offs. The portfolio reporting system should be flexible in providing adjusted cost basis for these types of activities. Capital gains reports and performance reports are enhancements available by some prime brokers.

PRIME BROKER FEES AND PERSONNEL

Fees for prime broker services will vary from firm to firm. There may be ticket costs on trades executed away and settled through the prime broker. This cost could range from zero to $25 per ticket. In some cases, a reduction in ticket

---

3. Carolyn Pope Keif, "What to Expect from a Premier Custodian," *Family Office Exchange,* December 1993.

expense is given if the advisor inputs trades via computer to the prime broker. A few prime brokers do not have a per-ticket cost, but may look for a percentage of the execution business to be placed through their trade desk. Most prime brokers have an independent trade desk to handle their clients' trades.

Experienced personnel at the prime broker are invaluable to the relationship between the advisor and the client and its master trustee bank. For some banks, market-neutral investing may be a new product. This could hold true also for the advisory firm adding the market-neutral advisor to staff. The prime broker should have knowledgeable people ready to assist, help educate on location, and respond quickly to inquiries. In new relationships, operational staff at the bank or advisor may have a difficult time understanding collateral cash versus investment cash. Utilizing an easy-to-understand portfolio system with a knowledgeable client service group, the prime broker should enhance the advisor/client relationship. Prime broker personnel should be easily accessible and stand ready to give efficient turn-around time to client request.

CONCLUSION

Take time to get input from the client, the trustee bank, and the advisor. Ask for references of clients utilizing market-neutral advisors and their advisors. This is a very important decision. Custodial issues are the responsibility of all parties involved in a market-neutral portfolio investment.

11

⑥ GLOBAL CUSTODY ISSUES

Richard Portogallo
Managing Director
Morgan Stanley & Co. Incorporated

In setting up a market-neutral fund or selecting a portfolio manager, sophisticated investors, multimanagers, and investment advisors spend a lot of time performing extensive analysis on the manager's strategy, risk controls, and historical returns. Often, however, they overlook a critical component of a successful global fund: the custodian or prime broker. In general, "custodian" and "prime broker" are used interchangeably. Poor selection of a prime broker may have as great an impact on a manager's performance as anything detailed previously in this book. We will spend the majority of this chapter identifying potential custody-related pitfalls and suggesting how to avoid them.

The impact of an inadequate global custodian is twofold. First, there is a direct economic loss to the fund from, for example, missed corporate actions and late settlements. Second, there is the opportunity cost. The managing general partner—the person in charge of the investment decisions—becomes distracted. Instead of spending most of his or her time on portfolio and investment decisions, the manager is bogged down in operational detail. The opportunity cost of time spent on operational and accounting issues instead of implementing the fund's strategy can be enormous.

Often, hedge fund managers come from a position in which they have enjoyed extensive back-office support. As a result, it was never necessary for them to deal with the day-to-day issues of trades failing or reports being delivered late. When they start a new fund, managers are faced not only with raising money, but also with making decisions about such basics as where to locate the office and how to track the fund's holdings. The general partner frequently engages a prime broker to act as an extension of the fund's back office, handling clearance and custody, financing, securities borrowing, and consolidated reporting.

Problems may arise when leveraged funds begin investing internationally while continuing to use the prime brokers they selected prior to investing abroad. Now they are faced with the myriad problems associated with clearing and settling trades and reporting in multiple currencies. A fund may be unable to settle in a particular market because its prime broker does not have an agent bank or is unable to borrow stock there. No matter how effective a prime broker may be in the United States, it simply may be unequipped to provide these services globally. Invariably, the performance of the fund could be adversely affected.

A review of the operational issues that may arise when investing internationally is intended to help market-neutral fund managers evaluate and monitor prime brokers and anticipate their internal operational needs. Knowledge of these issues will also assist investors in evaluating and monitoring a fund's operational and accounting controls and those of its service providers.

THE ROLE OF PRIME BROKERS

Prime brokerage operations were established by broker-dealers approximately 20 years ago in response to demand from hedge funds for a single firm to clear, custody, finance, and report on their trades with multiple executing brokers. Why use multiple executing brokers? The first reason is anonymity. The funds do not want their executing brokers to become too familiar with their positions or proprietary strategies. If others use the same strategy, it can make the required stocks too difficult to borrow or decrease the small price discrepancies on which the fund depends.

Another reason is to obtain stock in hot issues—those initial public offerings in which excess demand is likely to increase a stock several points as soon as it is issued. Executing brokers allocate their new-issue syndicate participation among their best customers. Hedge funds spread out commissions to multiple brokers in order to receive hot-deal stocks from each of them.

General partners also may spread around commission dollars in order to obtain research and related computer and data-retrieval services. These "soft dollar" payments are particularly valuable because fund managers attempt to keep their operations lean, and they lack the infrastructure to produce their own research.

And finally, hedge funds use multiple brokers to get the best-quality execution. Some firms may be stronger in over-the-counter equities, some in listed equities, some in derivatives. Hedge funds want to execute with whichever broker will get them the best execution for a particular transaction.

Working with all these firms creates a problem of control. If positions and balances were to be held at multiple brokerage houses, it would be difficult operationally to keep track of positions, performance, and corporate actions. In addition, it is more expensive to finance a number of smaller balances than a single large one. A global prime broker enables a fund to execute all over the world, while domiciling and financing its position at a single firm. The result is minimized operational headaches and financing costs. (See Figure 11–1.)

Regulation

Since its inception, the prime brokerage business has operated in a regulatory vacuum. Just two years ago, a group of

FIGURE 11-1

Information Flows

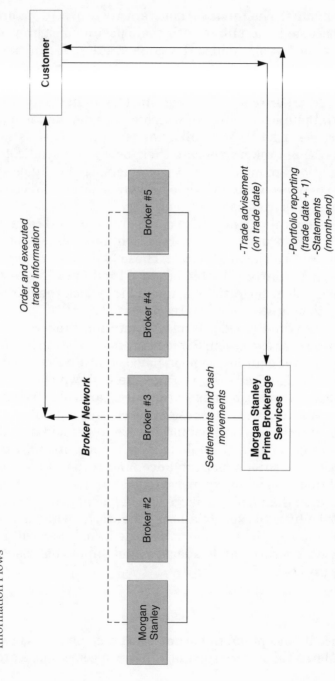

Source: Morgan Stanley & Co. Incorporated

brokers came together to eliminate some ambiguities associated with this business and to shape a regulatory framework. The Securities and Exchange Commission (SEC) ratified this framework by issuing a "no action" letter that became effective October 1, 1994.

One of the major areas of concern in the prime brokerage community has been which broker "owns" the trade. Is the executing broker or the prime broker responsible for paying up and collecting if the client cannot pay for a trade? The SEC essentially determined that if the prime broker does not DK or disaffirm a trade within 24 hours, it is responsible for the remainder of the settlement cycle. If the trade facts match between the executing broker and the prime broker, the transaction is automatically affirmed through the Depository Trust Company (DTC) Interactive ID system. However, the prime broker still has until noon on trade day plus one to disaffirm the trade for credit or margin reasons. This means the executing broker must do its homework to determine whether the customer can pay for a trade.

Other new regulations involve account size and documentation. In order to open a prime brokerage account, a registered investment advisor now must have U.S. $100,000 of equity; this increases to U.S. $500,000 for those that are not registered advisors. A series of documents and contracts have to be executed by executing brokers, prime brokers, and hedge funds to formalize a prime brokerage relationship.

Going Global

In the 1990s, many types of investment firms have entered the leveraged investing arena—often in an effort to keep their top managers from leaving to start hedge funds on their own. In order for these new structures to succeed, investment firms must turn to a prime broker for global margin financing, the securities borrowing services it needs to sell short, and other specialized products and services.

Prime brokers provide services similar to those provided by global custodians. The difference is that the prime broker can borrow securities for its clients, whereas global custodians—which operate as trust companies—are generally not permitted to do so.

Until the late 1980s, prime brokers provided a limited range of services to hedge funds and certain high-net-worth individuals. These services were clearance and custody of domestic securities, financing, reporting, and securities borrowing. Other investors such as mutual funds, pension funds, insurance companies, foundations and endowments, and asset management firms started to use short selling and leveraged strategies, they began using prime brokers and demanded from them the sorts of services they were accustomed to receiving from their global custodians. At the same time, hedge fund clients were moving abroad to take advantage of opportunities outside the United States. Some prime brokers built agent bank networks to provide international clearance and custody and such value-added services as tax reclaims, corporate actions, and dividend information.

The Hybrid Account

Despite the increasing similarity between the services provided by a prime broker and a bank or trust company, many entities still require a trust company or bank (see Table 11–1), as opposed to a broker-dealer, to act as custodian. The reasons vary and may range from perceptions or historical relationships to legal and regulatory requirements. This creates a challenge for financial institutions to offer such broker-dealer services as margin and securities lending while meeting the funds requirements of utilizing a trust company or bank. There are two commonly used mechanisms to facilitate such a hybrid.

Subcustody Agreement
A subcustody structure allows a client to appoint a broker-dealer as a subcustodian to a trust company master custo-

TABLE   11–1

Prime Brokerage versus Bank Custody

	Traditional Prime Brokerage	Bank Custody	Prime Brokerage in 1990s
Client bases			
• Asset management companies		X	X
• Foundations and endowments		X	X
• Hedge funds	X		X
• High-net-worth individuals	X	X	X
• Insurance companies		X	X
• Mutual funds		X	X
• Pension funds		X	X
Services			
• Agent bank network management		X	X
• Cash management		X	X
• Clearance and custody—domestic	X	X	X
• Clearance and custody—global		X	X
• Corporate actions reporting		X	X
• Financing—domestic	X		X
• Financing—global			X
• Foreign exchange		X	X
• Fund accounting		X	X
• Reporting/information distribution	X	X	X
• Securities borrowing (short sale processing)	X		X
• Securities lending, discretionary		X	X
• Tax reclamation		X	X

Source: Morgan Stanley & Co. Incorporated

dian. The fund's manager deals directly with the prime broker, which retains the assets and reports positions and activity to the bank or trust company, which in turn prepares the necessary reporting for the beneficial holder. The client continues to deal directly with and receive reports from its trust company or bank, maintaining consistency in its custody relationship.

Special Custody

The special custody structure enables a broker-dealer to hold a fund's short positions while a bank or trust company holds the long positions. The trust company holds the collateral against the short activity in a special holdings account in the name of the prime broker. This facility also allows the broker-dealer to extend credit, with securities collateralized in a special holdings account at the trust company. As this structure requires multiple agents and accounts, effective coordination among the client, fund manager, trust company, and prime broker is critical. When opting for this structure, select a prime broker and bank or trust company that has the experience and technology to facilitate it.

AGENT BANK EVALUATION

An international hedge fund requires a prime broker that is able not only to clear and settle in its time zone, but also to settle in multiple locations. While some major global custodians have branch banks in many countries, prime brokers—which are units of broker-dealers—do not. Instead, they provide broad market coverage through networks of agent banks. Morgan Stanley, for example, can settle trades in more than 55 countries through its network of agent banks. Additionally, we self-clear in France, Germany, Hong Kong, Japan, Switzerland, the United Kingdom, and the United States in order to control settlement costs in the highest-volume markets.

In order to maintain high service-levels, prime brokers must actively manage these agent banks or subcustodians, evaluating, among other things

- Their financial strength,
- Their commitment to the particular region and product;
- Their level of automation and sophistication;
- Their activity level within the marketplace (do they settle one trade a day or 500 trades a day?);

T A B L E   11–2

Agent Bank Network Management

Selection Criteria
- Creditworthiness
- Senior management commitment
- Quality of personnel
- Superior technology (SWIFT; proprietary system)
- Standards of care across categories (see below)
- Market share
- Reputation
- Cost

Standard of Care Categories
- Custody organization
- Securities processing
- Safekeeping functions
- Income and dividends collection
- Corporate actions
- Proxy voting
- Tax reclamation
- Securities transfer
- Cash management
- Communication processing
- Security control
- Data and reconciliation
- Data processing
- Audit and regulatory
- Insurance
- Fees and invoicing

Management Process
- Annual RFPs from all providers in market (helps benchmark current provider)
- Semiannual evaluations
- On-site due diligence reviews
- Statistical reporting: settlement date and broker
- Pricing

Source: Morgan Stanley & Co. Incorporated

- The quality of their personnel, their settlement statistics (e.g., are they failing on trade day plus one on 80 percent of the cases?);
- Their market share; and
- Their cost.

The prime broker must also evaluate the other banks in the country in order to create local benchmarks and select an alternate if the current agent falls short of the broker's service standards. The prime broker's network management staff should meet regularly with its distant agents to evaluate new functionalities and examine their procedures. Based on its findings, the staff then recommends either that the prime broker continue to do business with that agent bank or find another service provider. (See Table 11.2.)

To assess the performance of a prime broker, you will want to determine its procedures for monitoring its agent banks. You should request a list of the specific agent banks, along with some of its credit and evaluation reports, which will show how good the agent banks are relative to their competitors. It is also a good idea to compare your prime broker's list of agent banks with the rankings provided in many global custody magazines. The more information you can extract from the prime broker on its agent bank network, the better position you will be in internationally.

OPERATIONAL CHALLENGES

Qualified Investors

Many markets require investors or their prime brokers to register with the local governing bodies as qualified financial entities. If you choose not to register, you may still be able to trade in a market by utilizing the license of an executing broker, under a prearranged strategy. The disadvantage is that the local exchange will only recognize the executing broker as the owner of the securities. This makes you captive to that broker for execution and exposes you to broker risk. You would also be subject to the risks and complexities, mentioned earlier, associated with maintaining multiple custody relationships. For this reason, it is beneficial to determine in which markets you will be engaged and what form of preinvestment protocol would best suit your needs.

Transaction Costs

In the global markets, the cost of clearing is much greater than in the United States. Prime brokers usually charge between $15 and $25 per domestic transaction, or may waive the fee altogether if the fund's balances (debits, credits, and shorts) reach a certain level. Internationally, costs are typically higher; in fact, it is extremely expensive to clear in markets that are less developed. These markets are often physical in nature rather than book entry, and settlement requires a tremendous amount of manual intervention. The agent banks do this work, but then pass along the costs to the prime broker. The cost per transaction can be as high as $200.

It is important to analyze the cost of clearing before allocating capital to a strategy, particularly a high-volume strategy. Let us say you are contemplating a quantitative equity long/short strategy in Southeast Asia with 100 percent turnover that requires a quarterly or a monthly rebalancing. The clearance costs associated with such a strategy could be substantial enough to impact the performance of the fund.

If your prime broker has good international execution capabilities, you may be able to control clearance fees by executing trades with that firm. Prime brokers will sometimes waive clearance fees when they execute the trades.

Contractual Settlement

In international markets you also face the possibility of dealing in a noncontractual settlement environment. In the United States, virtually all transactions are settled on a contractual basis (not to be confused with guaranteed settlement): You buy or sell a security, and on settlement date your account is charged or credited with the cash for the settlement regardless of whether your prime broker receives the securities from or delivers them to its counterparty. This practice facilitates cash management, enabling a fund's manager to count on having money or securities in an account on a certain date. In the international markets you may be dealing in an actual—not contractual—settlement environment, in which cash is charged or credited when a trade actually settles. In such situations, managers risk becoming hostage to their prime broker's inefficiencies in delivering or receiving securities. If a prime broker has inadequate experience in Southeast Asia and has a 50 percent fail rate in Malaysia, the manager cannot know when he or she will receive cash from a sale of securities.

Foreign Exchange

You must also consider the foreign exchange component of cross-border transactions. Essentially, there are two ways to settle a multicurrency trade: through dollars and through local currency.

Dollar Settlement

The advantage of settling a transaction in dollars is simply that it is easier. The manager receives a dollar price quote from the executing broker, which he or she reports to the prime broker, which books a dollar trade through its processing systems. The transaction settles in dollars.

However, there are a number of disadvantages in dealing with a dollar settlement. One is settlement risk. Because these markets are usually not delivery versus payment (DVP), you deliver stock free abroad and receive payment separately in the United States. If the broker becomes insolvent, you may never get paid.

The other disadvantage of dealing in dollars is that you lose control of the cost of the transaction. Foreign exchange in itself is a transaction with associated costs. When you settle in dollars, you basically give the executing broker the right to price the foreign exchange rate at the level it chooses.

Dealing in Local Currency
One advantage of dealing in local currency when settling transactions internationally is that you reduce the settlement risk. Everything is done on a DVP basis. You'll also gain more flexibility in terms of pricing the transaction, and you can deal with any foreign exchange broker, not just the executing broker, so you can shop for a good rate. Another advantage is that you can actually wait until settlement date to do the foreign exchange trade. Instead of going into the forward market and doing it on trade day, you can execute the foreign exchange in the spot market if you choose to take some currency risk.

The major disadvantage of trading in local currency is that it is somewhat more complicated. It requires someone from the fund or its prime broker to keep track of the settlements that are expected each day and to roll them up to have one firm execute the foreign exchange contract. This requires systems at both the prime broker and the fund that enable them to monitor multicurrency cash flows.

No-Fail Markets

Certain markets levy significant fees and other sanctions for failing. In the United States, it is possible for a transaction to fail for a few days without any adverse result—the stop-gap being that the prime broker will borrow the security in order to make delivery, limiting the likelihood of buy-ins. In many international markets, the likelihood of buy-ins is much greater because many jurisdictions levy fees and fines for open fails, and some markets impose mandatory buy-ins. The risk of buy-ins is compounded by restrictions or supply constraints that may make it impossible for a prime broker to borrow the security. I can recall a situation in Malaysia in which a counterparty failed to deliver a security to Morgan Stanley and the exchange automatically closed out the client's position on trade date plus one. Adding insult to injury, communication of such closeouts may be delayed, so that you may not find out until days, sometimes weeks, later that a trade has been bought in.

To protect investors from the cost and consequences of failure, some prime brokers offer auto-borrow facilities. Auto-borrow means that if the prime broker recognizes that a trade is going to fail, it will go out and borrow that security on behalf of the customer and make the delivery, thereby avoiding sanctions, fees, and automatic buy-ins.

Registration

In order for you to collect dividends in many markets, the security you own must be registered in the name of the beneficial owner or the nominee of the firm that is holding the security on the fund's behalf. The mechanisms for registration often are manual, requiring the physical security to be sent to a registrar or transfer agent for up to eight weeks or more. (In India, registration can take up to six months.) Investors cannot sell securities when they are out for registration without borrowing the stock. In cases of hard-to-borrow stocks or in markets in which borrowing securities is prohibited, you can be hamstrung in your ability to sell a particular security because the stock is out for dividend registration.

It is essential, therefore, for portfolio managers and traders to know when securities will be out for registration. If you have a prime broker, it should provide this information. It is important also that funds understand their prime brokers' registration procedures. Some prime brokers will send securities out to be reregistered without client instruction once the stock settles. Others will do it in bulk right before the registration period. Others will wait until they are notified in writing by their customer. When a security has a relatively low dividend, a manager may decide it is better not to register it at all in order to preserve the flexibility to sell it at any time. An understanding of these procedures and their consequences is essential. Fortunately, markets generally are moving away from physical securities to scripless systems such as in Japan and the United States.

Tax Reclaims

Of all the facets of global investment processing, tax reclamation may be the single area in which practitioners have made the least headway. Under the terms of tax treaties between the United States and other countries, investors may have the right to reclaim taxes withheld on a transaction or income distribution. However, reclamation procedures are often complex. Some banks and a few prime brokers currently handle the tax reclaim process for their clients.

Reclamation is generally smoothest in countries with centralized administration for the handling of claims by foreign investors. In the absence of a centralized facility, claims for tax relief are usually referred to the regional tax office that handles the affairs of the issuing entity. Unfortunately, regional tax offices within one country may be inconsistent with respect to their requirements, making compliance more difficult. Even where properly documented tax procedures are in place, variations in interpretation may occur.

Finding solutions to international tax recovery problems requires the collective effort of the investors, prime brokers, international clearing agents, and the tax authorities. Although often misunderstood, tax reclaims are a source of income that should not be overlooked. (See Table 11–3.)

MULTICURRENCY REPORTING

Reports on cash and positions are typically generated in a batch overnight environment from the prime broker's system and delivered electronically or physically to the fund

TABLE 11-3

Dividend Tax Reclaims Statute of Limitations Table

Country of Residence

Country of issue	at source	Australia	Belgium	Canada	France	Germany	Italy	Japan	Lux	Netherlands	New Zealand	U.K.	U.S.
Austria_a	N	5	3	5	3	5	5	5	2	3	n/a	3	5
Belgium_a	N	3	n/a	3	3	3	3	3	3	3	3	3	3
Canada_a	Y	2	2	n/a	2	2	2	2	2	2	2	2	2
Denmark_b	N	20	20	20	20	2	20	20	20	20	20	20	20
Finland_d	Y	5	5	5	5	5	5	5	5	5	5	5	5
France_ac	N	2	2	2	n/a	2	2	2	2	2	2	2	2
Germany_a	N	4	4	4	4	n/a	4	4	4	4	4	4	4
Italy_d	N	1.5	1.5	1.5	1.5	1.5	n/a	1.5	1.5	1.5	1.5	1.5	1.5
Netherlands_a	N	3	2	3	3	5	5	5	3	n/a	5	6	3
Norway_a	Y	<20	<20	<20	<20	<20	<20	<20	<20	<20	<20	<20	<20
Portugal_d	N	4	4	4	4	4	4	4	4	4	4	4	4
Spain_a	N	1	1e	1	1f	1e	1	1	1	2e	n/a	2g	1
Sweden_a	Y	5	5	5	5	5	5	5	5	5	5	5	5
Switzerland_a	N	3	3	3	3	3	3	3	3	2	3	3	3
U.K._a	N	6	6	6	6	6	6	6	6	6	6	6	6

All amounts are in years unless otherwise indicated.

a. This deadline is calculated from the end of the calendar year during which the dividend was paid.

b. This deadline is calculated from the end of the calendar year during which the dividend was paid unless the bond owner is German, in which case the deadline is calculated from the dividend payment date.

c. The actual French statute states one year, but market practice is two years.

d. This deadline is calculated from the dividend payment date.

e. This deadline is from the twentieth day of the first month following the calendar month in which the dividend was paid.

g. This deadline is calculated from the end of the calendar year in which tax was withheld.

This table is a quick reference guide only. It is based on information believed to be accurate at the date indicated on this publication (May 28, 1995).

Source: Morgan Stanley Trust Company.

192

on trade date plus one. Essentially, these daily position and profit and loss (P&L) reports inform the general partner or the accounting or operational people within that particular hedge fund about the portfolio holdings within that particular strategy. The reports indicate what the fund's inventory is, mark the inventory to the market, and segregate inventory based on asset class, strategies or styles, and security descriptions.

International funds also require multicurrency reports that value portfolios in local currencies and a base currency. To produce these reports, the prime broker must be able to price securities in many markets accurately and regularly and lock in foreign exchange rates for cash.

Investor Reports

Recently, some institutions have asked investment managers to open up separately managed accounts and to provide the institution with the prime broker's reports on a daily, weekly, or as-needed basis. This permits the investing institution to monitor performance more closely than is possible with the quarterly summary reports that hedge funds traditionally prepare for investors. Position reports also enable investors to hedge some of a fund manager's strategies.

Of course, managers do have good reasons not to provide investors with detailed reports more frequently than quarterly. First, it may simply be overkill. Second, the managers may be concerned that the investor will use the information to piggyback off of what the managers feel are proprietary strategies. If others employ the same strategy, that can hurt the fund's performance.

Corporate Actions

In addition to position and P&L reports, the prime broker also provides hedge funds with reports regarding corporate actions. These reports indicate such things as which stocks are going ex-dividend, what items are being paid on a particular date, and what items are out for registration so they cannot be sold. The prime broker accesses data from a number of vendors to get this information, runs it through the portfolio system as a filter, and then produces reports for each customer based on the portfolio holdings.

OFFSHORE FINANCING

Prime brokers play a more active role in assessing credit risk outside the United States. When a prime broker lends money in the United States, it is generally subject to Regulation "T", which limits margin lending to a customer to 50 percent of the value of the securities in its account. That's a big cushion. If a security's price drops, there is usually plenty of time to obtain money from customers to get their collateral back up to house requirements, which are often less than 50 percent, or, if necessary, to liquidate the security to retrieve the loaned money.

In the international markets, the absence of Regulation "T" means that managers are subject to their prime broker's appetite for how much leverage it wants to provide, based on a strategy and the risk associated with it, with the floor being set by such local regulatory bodies as the U. K. Securities and Futures Authority (SFA). This means a customer can execute a strategy outside the United States at the same margin requirements under which a proprietary broker-dealer operates; it is simply a function of how comfortable the prime broker is with the counterparty and its positions and with monitoring the strategy.

How does the prime broker determine how much it makes sense to lend? First, it will look at the strategy, running it through different risk systems it has developed. Then it will recommend haircut levels for each security or type of security. If it is a market-neutral strategy, for example, the prime broker might recommend haircuts based on volatility, tracking from the portfolio, and various other measures. If it is a convertible bond arbitrage strategy it may recommend haircuts based on the amount of premium in the bond, whether the bond is hedged or unhedged on a parity or delta basis, and on how difficult it is to convert the bond into the underlying equity in the event that the prime broker needs to do so to meet its borrowing obligation.

The result is that the margin process becomes another area of negotiation with which the manager must deal for offshore accounts. Not only are you negotiating the financing rates for that particular strategy, you are also negotiating with the prime broker what the haircuts would be. It is important to understand the legal and regulatory considerations because not every fund is eligible to be carried on the books of a foreign broker-dealer. You should be familiar with these restrictions and regulations before you decide to embark on the strategy.

In an international context, each market-neutral fund's strategy raises different credit issues and presents different risks to the lender. Here are examples of the issues with respect to convertible bond and equity arbitrage strategies.

Convertible Bond Arbitrage

One issue associated with how much credit a prime broker is willing to extend, particularly on the books of a foreign broker-dealer, is how easily convertible the underlying stock is. If it is a name that can be converted in two to three days, that clearly reduces the risk profile of the entity extending credit for the prime broker. If it may take three to four weeks to convert, that tends to increase the haircut on that particular position because the prime broker now assumes additional risk.

The risk lies in the possibility that the short security will be recalled (that is, the institution that is lending it to the prime broker wants the stock back), and the prime broker won't be able to deliver the stock back in time. When this happens, the institution buys in the short stock and automatically closes the transaction. If you are long a bond and you lose the offset short against it, you have effectively lifted a leg—removed one of two sides of a hedge—increasing your risk to the position, and your prime broker's risk, as well. In normal situations, the prime broker will attempt to reborrow the stock. If it is unable to do so, it instructs the hedge fund to convert the bond into the underlying shares and deliver the shares back to the lender. A loss may occur if, for example, it takes five weeks to convert the bond and the lender needed the stock back in two days. Therefore, of concern to the prime broker is both the liquidity of the short and how long it will take to convert the long bond, if it can be converted at all.

Equity Arbitrage

If an equity arbitrage strategy is executed on the books of a broker-dealer in the United States, Regulation "T" generally requires the prime broker to collect 50 percent on both the long and short sides (assuming margin eligibility), so you can only lever up the portfolio two to one. On a foreign broker-dealer's books, on the other hand, you can lever that strategy up to the broker-dealer's appetite for leverage to get potentially more performance out of it. However, this increased leverage adds incrementally to the risk of the strategy. That is why it is so important for investors to understand just how much leverage the manager is using. If the manager is using extraordinary amounts of leverage to try to enhance his returns, it could become a risk strategy.

INTERNATIONAL SECURITIES LENDING

A major component of the prime brokerage service is securities lending. This service enables the customer to short securities by selling and delivering to the buyer securities it does not own. It is important that a prime broker be able to borrow securities in every market in which a fund wants to trade. In markets with short settlement cycles or in which the cost of fails is high, borrows frequently are needed to make delivery, as well as to cover short sales.

Securities Lending Mechanics

When a manager shorts a security, it calls the prime broker to "obtain a locate on"—or find—the required stock to borrow. The prime broker's securities lending group will generally first check its own box to see whether the stock is available. A firm's box combines its proprietary trading accounts and customer accounts running debit balances, including other hedge fund accounts. Under a "hypothecation agreement" and SEC rules, brokers are permitted to lend out 140 percent of a customer's debit balance in order to finance that debit. Borrowing internally is usually most cost-effective, enabling the prime broker to pass a higher rebate on to its customer.

If a prime broker does not have a stock internally, it looks to its institutional network, which includes banks and other large institutional holders that have discretionary lending programs. As a final option, the prime broker will borrow stock from other broker-dealers. Although broker-dealers may offer better rebate rates than do institutions, they are a less desirable source because their loans are less stable. Broker-dealers are subject to customer segmentation requirements, under which they have to "lock up" certain securities nightly according to a sophisticated algorithm. If a broker has to lock up stock it has borrowed, it must relocate the security or call it back from its customer. If it recalls the stock, the customer has to unwind its arbitrage or other strategy, effectively giving up the money it hoped to earn. Institutions, on the other hand, only recall loaned securities when they sell them.

The prime broker produces and distributes daily reports informing the manager of the cost of borrowing particular securities. The prime broker should also report any fee changes on a daily basis.

Supply

Before executing a particular strategy, assess the borrowing capabilities of your prime broker in the region. If your prime broker lacks institutional relationships within a particular region, you'll need to open up an account with a broker that does. This leaves you open to the risks of unbundling discussed earlier in this chapter. That is why it makes sense prior to choosing your prime broker to figure out what your strategies are going to be on the short side and where you potentially will be executing these transactions.

Legal Status

Another thing you want to ascertain beforehand are the legalities of shorting securities in a particular market. In the United Kingdom, for example, the only way to gain short-side exposure is through what they call contracts for differences (CFDs), which essentially are equity swaps. Since the equity swap tends not to be a clearinghouse-eligible product, which means that it cannot be cleared from one firm to another, you will have to execute the strategy with the firm that provides you with the CFD.

Pricing

The cost to borrow securities in international markets is a function of supply, as it is in the United States, and of the size of the position. Note that when you lend cash and borrow securities in the United States, you receive a "rebate" priced off of Fed funds or the broker call rate. Elsewhere, you receive a fee.

Some equity market-neutral funds start with small amounts of capital to enable the manager to develop a track record. This means the manager is trading very small lots of particular securities in certain countries. But if you are dealing in less than 1,000-share lots in Japan, the cost to borrow is extremely high because institutions are unenthusiastic about lending small lots of stock, and charge accordingly for the nuisance. It is common when you are dealing in very small lots, therefore, for rebates to be minimal or nonexistent. For this reason, the size of your strategy should be discussed in advance with your prime broker.

TABLE 11-4

Summary Checklist of International Operations Issues

- Agent bank network
  Quality by country
  Breadth
  Monitoring process
- Investor qualification requirements by country
- Transaction costs by country
- Foreign exchange: dealing in dollars versus local currency
- Penalties for fails by country; custodian's auto-borrow facilities
- Dividend registration
  Requirements by country
  Custodian's procedures
- Multicurrency reporting
- Corporate actions
  Tracking methods and sources
  Reporting
- Offshore financing
  Haircuts
  Rates
  Risk management
- Securities lending (by country)
  Supply
  Legalities
  Pricing

Source: Morgan Stanley & Co. Incorporated

CONCLUSION

Global investing presents a wealth of operational and accounting challenges—along with a wealth of investment opportunity (see Table 11–4). To maximize the opportunities, market-neutral funds should prepare to meet the challenges at the outset. Selecting a global prime broker is a first step toward ensuring efficient access to all the markets in which you want—or will want—to participate, keeping tight control via multicurrency and corporate actions reports, leveraging performance via financing, and maximizing short-sale potential through cost-effective securities lending. It is also important that the fund have some infrastructure and expertise internally, at the very least to monitor the performance of its prime broker.

Finally, when selecting a prime broker, hiring operations and accounting staff, and establishing internal procedures, keep in mind that your ultimate goal is to enable the fund's manager to concentrate on investment decisions. For while poor operational and accounting controls can hurt performance, it is sound strategies and effective implementation that drive performance.

INDEX